Ninja CREAMi Culinary Adventures Cookbook:

Your Ultimate Frozen Dessert Recipe Book
for Crafting Perfect Ice creams, Milkshakes,
Sorbets, Gelato, and other sweets

Christmas Edition

By GALE COOKE

TABLE OF CONTENTS

INTRODUCTION

Welcome to the Summer Edition of the "Ninja CREAMi Culinary Adventures Cookbook," a refreshed and vibrant guide to mastering the art of frozen desserts with your beloved Ninja CREAMi. This edition isn't just a sequel; it's a celebration of summer flavors, an anthology of recipes that have been specially chosen to complement the warmth and joy of the season.

The Ninja CREAMi, a marvel of kitchen technology, continues to stand at the forefront of our culinary adventures. Its unparalleled ease of use and versatility are what make this cookbook's summer edition possible, allowing us to explore an even wider array of frozen delights tailored for the season. Picture the silkiest mango gelatos, the most refreshing watermelon sorbets, and smoothie bowls bursting with the flavors of summer berries – each recipe is a testament to the endless possibilities afforded by the Ninja CREAMi.

Designed to cater to both the experienced chef and the curious novice, this edition builds on the foundation of our original collection. We've listened to our readers – yes, you! – incorporating your invaluable feedback to enhance every aspect of this book. From adding handy tags, to an entire new chapter dedicated to summer recipes. Everything to make sure you can choose a recipe that suits your diet and enjoy the hot summer days.

This book goes beyond being a mere collection of recipes; it's a guide to embracing the season's spirit in your culinary creations. We dive deep into the art of balancing flavors, ensuring that the natural sweetness of summer fruits shines through in every bite. Texture contrasts, from creamy to icy, and presentation aesthetics, with vibrant colors that mirror the season's energy, are explored to inspire you to create desserts that are not only delicious but also visually stunning.

We understand the importance of accommodating diverse dietary needs, which is why this edition features an array of options for everyone. From decadent treats to health-conscious alternatives, each recipe comes with detailed nutritional information, empowering you to make choices that align with your dietary goals and preferences.

In these pages, you'll find recipes and a wealth of information about the Ninja CREAMi itself – from understanding its components and functionalities to mastering its various settings. We aim to make you comfortable and familiar with your Ninja CREAMi, making it an indispensable ally in your culinary adventures.

As we embark on this seasonal culinary adventure, we invite you to embrace the vibrant, flavorful world of summer with open arms. Let your imagination run wild, experiment with seasonal produce, and explore new textures and flavors. The Ninja CREAMi is your companion on this journey, ready to transform your summer inspirations into delicious realities.

So, with excitement and anticipation, let's turn the page and dive into our culinary journey. Here's to a season filled with sweet discoveries, shared moments, and the pure joy of home-made frozen desserts. Cheers to making this summer your most delicious one yet with your Ninja CREAMi!

GETTING TO KNOW NINJA CREAMI

What is Ninja CREAMi

The Ninja CREAMi represents a significant leap in home dessert-making technology. SharkNinja, known for its commitment to innovation in the household appliance sector, has always focused on creating products that simplify and enhance the culinary experience for home cooks. The company's entry into the frozen dessert maker market was no exception.

The Ninja CREAMi was introduced as a response to the growing trend of homemade, healthy, and customizable frozen desserts. Before its advent, making ice cream, gelato, sorbets, and similar desserts at home required either manual effort with essential tools or bulky, often expensive, ice cream makers that needed to be more versatile and required pre-freezing of ingredients or components.

What set the Ninja CREAMi apart was its revolutionary technology that transformed virtually any frozen solid into a creamy, smooth dessert with just a button. This appliance allowed users to turn frozen fruits into sorbets, mix in sweet treats to create ice creams or blend nuts and milk for healthier alternatives without needing pre-frozen bowls or lengthy preparation times.

One of the most significant innovations of the Ninja CREAMi is its ability to break down and mix frozen ingredients thoroughly, creating a texture that rivals professional-grade machines. This feature opened up new possibilities for creativity in the kitchen, allowing home cooks to experiment with flavors and ingredients that were previously difficult to work with in traditional ice cream makers.

The versatility, ease of use, and the ability to create healthier alternatives to store-bought desserts quickly made the Ninja CREAMi a favorite among health-conscious consumers and dessert enthusiasts alike. It became trendy among families, fitness enthusiasts, and those with dietary restrictions, allowing for complete control over the ingredients used in their frozen treats.

Why Choose Ninja CREAMi

The Ninja CREAMi is more than just a kitchen gadget; it's a revolutionary tool that has transformed how we think about and prepare frozen desserts.

Redefining Frozen Desserts: The Ninja CREAMi goes above and beyond traditional frozen dessert preparation. It doesn't just freeze ingredients; it churns them into creamy, dreamy treats. Its versatility shines as it effortlessly creates a spectrum of desserts, from rich ice creams and silky gelatos to light sorbets and thick milkshakes, surpassing the one-note performance of conventional ice cream makers.

Unmatched Versatility and Creativity: This device is unparalleled in its ability to process a wide variety of ingredients, inviting you to explore a plethora of unique flavor profiles and textures. Whether you're aiming to replicate a classic favorite or innovate with avant-garde combinations, the Ninja CREAMi is your companion in culinary creativity.

Simplicity and Accessibility: The Ninja CREAMi boasts user-friendly controls and clear settings, making the art of dessert-making approachable for all, regardless of cooking experience. Its intuitive operation ensures that creating frozen desserts becomes a straightforward and delightful endeavor for chefs at every level.

A Gateway to Healthier Options: For those mindful of their dietary intake, the Ninja CREAMi is a treasure. It empowers users to produce healthier alternatives to store-bought desserts, offering low-sugar, dairy-free, and fruit-based options that cater to a wide array of dietary requirements and preferences.

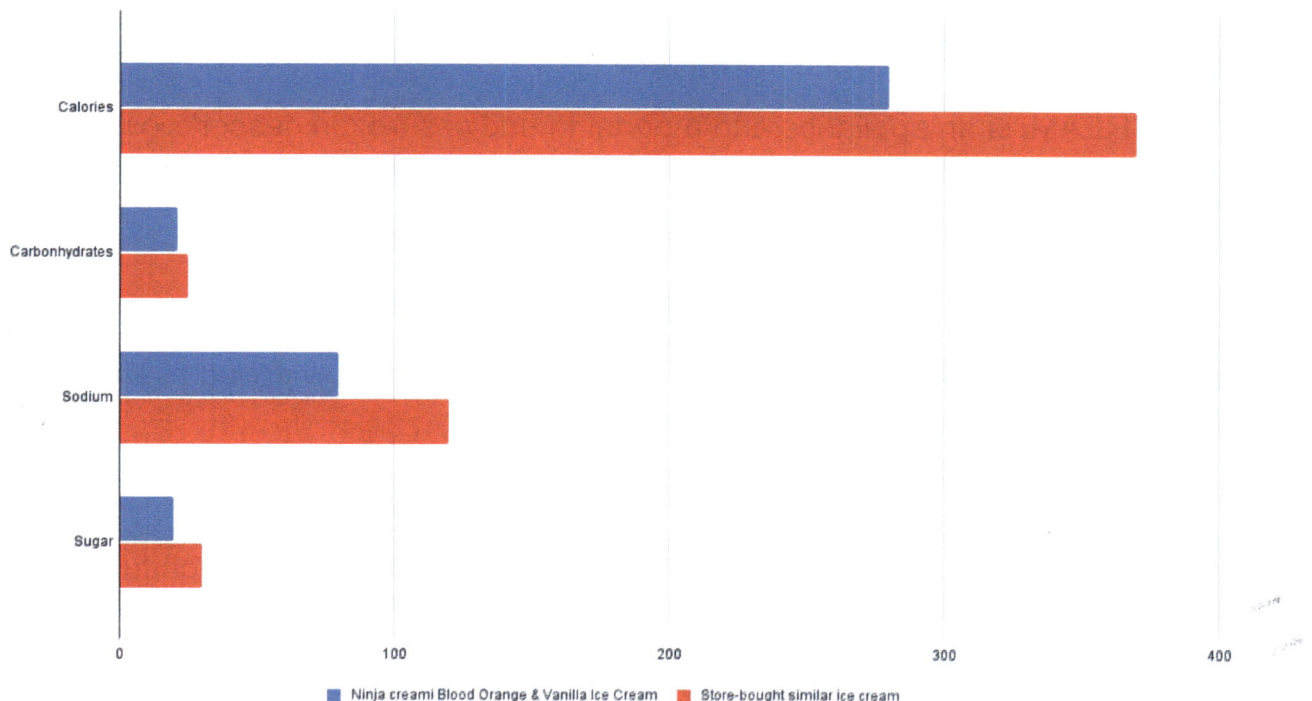

Legend: ■ Ninja creami Blood Orange & Vanilla Ice Cream ■ Store-bought similar ice cream

Store-bought ice creams often have a higher calorie and sugar content due to added preservatives and flavor enhancers. Additionally, they may include stabilizers and emulsifiers not present in homemade recipes, which can affect the nutritional profile slightly. The sodium content can also be higher in commercial products to enhance flavor and shelf life.

Sleek Design and Superior Functionality: With its contemporary, compact appearance, the Ninja CREAMi is designed to complement any kitchen aesthetic. Its durable components and easy-to-clean nature guarantee a hassle-free dessert-making process, merging style with functionality.

Pioneering Technology: The heart of the Ninja CREAMi is its innovative technology, which ensures consistently smooth and creamy results, setting it apart from competitors. This technological excellence is a testament to SharkNinja's dedication to pushing the boundaries of home appliance innovation.

Exclusive Features Setting It Apart:

- Custom Freeze Technology: Unlike other makers, the Ninja CREAMi features a unique freeze mechanism that caters to the perfect texture for each dessert type, offering unmatched customization.
- Pre-set Programs for Precision: With specialized programs for each dessert category, the Ninja CREAMi removes the guesswork, ensuring perfect outcomes every time.
- Smart Ingredient Recognition: Innovative sensors adjust the churning process based on the ingredient composition, a feature not found in conventional machines.
- Eco-Friendly Operation: The Ninja CREAMi is designed with energy efficiency in mind, consuming less power compared to its peers, making it a greener choice for environmentally conscious users.
- Comprehensive Support and Community: Owning a Ninja CREAMi grants access to an exclusive community of enthusiasts and a wealth of online resources, providing inspiration and support that goes beyond the manual.

The Ninja CREAMi is an appliance and a portal to endless frozen dessert possibilities. It's an essential tool for anyone exploring the delightful world of homemade frozen treats with ease and versatility.

Getting Started

Here's a quick guide to help you understand its components, how it works, and the delicious meals you can prepare with it.

Ninja Cream Components

Let's explore the critical components of the Ninja CREAMi, each thoughtfully designed to make creating frozen treats at home both easy and enjoyable.

- Motor Base: The core of the Ninja CREAMi, housing the motor and control panel with various function settings for frozen treats.
- Creamerizer Paddle: Essential for blending and churning frozen ingredients into a smooth texture, this paddle is central to Ninja CREAMi's functionality.
- CREAMi Pints: Freezer-safe containers used to freeze ingredients before processing. Each pint is equipped with a lid for easy storage.
- Outer Bowl and Lid: Holds the CREAMi Pint during processing. The outer bowl ensures the pint stays in place, while the lid covers the assembly for safety and efficiency.
- Control Panel: Located on the motor base, it features buttons for different dessert settings, making the operation straightforward and user-friendly.

How It Works

The Ninja CREAMi operates on a simple yet effective principle. You prepare your dessert mixture (such as fruit purees, cream bases, etc.) and pour it into the CREAMi Pint. After freezing the pint for about 24 hours, insert it into the Ninja CREAMi with the Creamerizer Paddle attached. The appliance then processes the frozen block, churning and scraping it into a creamy, smooth consistency.

Ninja CREAMi Functions

The Ninja CREAMi elevates the art of frozen dessert creation, offering specialized functions to cater to every taste and dietary preference. Here's an expanded look at each function, guiding you on when to use them, the best ingredients to pair, and a glance at nutritional variations.

Ice Cream Function: This setting is your go-to for crafting both timeless and imaginative ice cream flavors. It excels with a base of cream and sugar but is equally adept with alternatives like coconut milk for dairy-free versions. Opt for this when craving a classic dessert experience, balancing sweetness and creaminess. Nutritional info will vary; traditional recipes may be higher in fat and calories, while substitutions like almond milk can offer lighter options.

Gelato Function: Choose gelato for a denser, more flavorful treat. This function shines with high-quality milk and less air, producing a richer texture. It's perfect for those afternoons when you crave an indulgent, artisanal dessert. Gelato typically has less fat than ice cream but compensates with a more intense flavor and a smoother feel.

Sorbet Function: Ideal for dairy-free and fruit-centric desserts, the sorbet setting turns frozen fruits and sweeteners into luscious, icy treats. It's best when seeking a palate cleanser or a light dessert option that's low in fat and calories but rich in fruit flavors. Sorbets are a fantastic choice for those managing dairy restrictions or looking for a refreshing dessert with lower calorie content.

Smoothie Bowl Function: This feature is perfect for creating nutritious, spoonable delights. It blends thicker than traditional smoothies, using frozen fruits, vegetables, and add-ins like protein powders or nuts. Opt for this as a fulfilling breakfast or a rejuvenating snack, offering a balance of vitamins, proteins, and fibers with adjustable sweetness levels.

Milkshake Function: When desiring a decadent, sippable treat, the milkshake setting is unmatched. It works best with ice cream or frozen yogurt and milk, creating a rich, creamy texture. This function is ideal for special occasions or as an indulgent reward, generally higher in calories and sugar, depending on your choice of milk and ice cream.

Lite Ice Cream Function: This mode allows for lower calorie and fat versions of your favorite ice creams. Using skim milk, alternative sweeteners, or fruit purées, you can enjoy a guilt-free version of classic flavors. Choose this when you're mindful of caloric intake but still wish for a creamy texture. Nutritionally, lite ice cream is a healthier alternative, reducing fat and sugar content without sacrificing satisfaction.

Mix-In Function: After the base of your frozen dessert is set, this function lets you incorporate chunky ingredients like nuts, chocolate chips, or berries. It ensures even distribution without crushing these add-ins, perfect for when you want added texture and flavor bursts in every bite. Nutritional additions will depend on the mix-ins chosen, allowing for customization according to dietary preferences or nutritional goals.

Re-Spin Function: If the initial texture isn't exactly as you hoped, the Re-Spin function is there for a do-over, ensuring your dessert reaches perfection. It's particularly useful for adjusting consistency or fully integrating flavors from late mix-ins. This function offers a way to fine-tune your desserts without significantly altering their nutritional profile.

Whether you're in the mood for a rich gelato, a refreshing sorbet, a nourishing smoothie bowl, or a classic milkshake, the Ninja CREAMi is your go-to solution for all things frozen and delightful. Enjoy exploring the endless possibilities that this incredible appliance offers!

The Building Blocks of Delicious Desserts

Creating delectable desserts with your Ninja CREAMi starts with choosing the right ingredients. Here's a guide to some fundamental building blocks that you can use to craft a wide variety of frozen treats:

Base Ingredients:

- Cream and Milk: For traditional ice creams and gelatos, heavy cream, whole milk, or half-and-half provide a rich, creamy texture.
- Dairy Alternatives: Almond milk, coconut milk, soy milk, or oat milk are great for vegan or lactose-intolerant options.
- Fruit Purees: Pureed fruits like berries, mangoes, or peaches are essential for sorbets and can be used in smoothie bowls.

Sweeteners:

- Sugar: Regular granulated sugar is a staple sweetener for many frozen desserts.
- Honey, Maple Syrup, or Agave: Natural sweeteners are excellent alternatives to refined sugar and can add distinct flavors.
- Sugar Substitutes: Artificial sweeteners or natural sugar substitutes like stevia can be used as a lower-calorie option.

Flavor Enhancers:

- Vanilla Extract: A dash of vanilla can enhance almost any dessert.
- Cocoa Powder or Chocolate: Cocoa powder or melted chocolate are vital ingredients for chocolate-based desserts.
- Coffee or Espresso: To add a coffee flavor, especially in gelatos.
- Citrus Zest or Juice: Lemon, lime, orange zest, and juice can add a refreshing tang to your desserts.

Mix-Ins:

- Nuts and Seeds: Almonds, pistachios, walnuts, or chia seeds can add crunch and nutrition.
- Chocolate Chips or Chunks: For a bit of chocolatey texture.
- Fruit Pieces: Fresh or dried fruit like berries, banana slices, or raisins can be mixed in for extra flavor and texture.
- Cookie or Cake Pieces: Adding crushed cookies or cake pieces can create fun and indulgent desserts.

Special Ingredients:

- Protein Powders: For a protein boost, especially in smoothie bowls.
- Yogurt or Greek Yogurt: Adds a tangy flavor and creamy texture.
- Spices and Herbs: Cinnamon, nutmeg, mint, or basil can infuse your desserts with unique flavors.

Thickeners:

- Cornstarch or Xanthan Gum: Useful for adding body to your desserts, especially in dairy-free or low-fat recipes.

Combining these ingredients in various proportions and experimenting with different flavor profiles allows you to use your Ninja CREAMi to create an endless array of frozen desserts tailored to your taste preferences and dietary needs. From classic favorites to innovative creations, the possibilities are limitless.

Tips and Tricks

Creating delicious desserts with your Ninja CREAMi can be an exciting and rewarding experience. Here are some tips and tricks to help you make the most out of your Ninja CREAMi and ensure your frozen treats turn out perfectly every time:

1   Start with Cold Ingredients: For best results, start with already cold ingredients. This helps the mixture freeze more uniformly and quickly in the CREAMi Pints.

2   Proper Freezing is Key: Ensure your mixture is fully frozen, ideally for 24 hours, before processing it in the Ninja CREAMi. Incomplete freezing can result in a less-than-ideal texture.

3   Fill to the Right Level: Avoid overfilling the CREAMi Pints. Stick to the MAX Fill line to ensure enough space for the mixture to churn properly without overflowing.

4   Balance Sweetness and Flavor: Remember that freezing dulls sweetness and flavors slightly, so your base mixture should be a tad sweeter and more flavorful than you want your final product to be.

5   Use Creamerizer Paddle Correctly: Always ensure the Creamerizer Paddle is correctly attached for efficient processing. This provides a smooth, even texture to your desserts.

6   Experiment with Mix-Ins: Add mix-ins like nuts, chocolate chips, or fruit pieces for texture and flavor. Use the Mix-In function to incorporate these elements without over-processing them.

7   Utilize the Re-Spin Function: If the texture isn't perfect on the first try, use the Re-Spin function. It can help achieve a smoother consistency or better integrate added ingredients.

8   Pre-Chill the Pints: Chill the CREAMi Pints in the freezer before adding your mixture. It can help speed up the freezing process.

9   Clean Promptly and Properly: Clean your Ninja CREAMi components immediately after use to prevent any residues from hardening, making them easier to clean.

10   Be patient with complex Mixes: Give the Ninja CREAMi more time to work magic if your mixture is challenging. More complex mixtures might take slightly longer to reach the perfect consistency.

11   Creative Flavor Combinations: Don't be afraid to experiment with unique flavor combinations. The Ninja CREAMi is perfect for culinary experimentation.

12   Layer Flavors for Complexity: Consider layering your ingredients when preparing the base mixture for a more complex flavor profile.

13   Monitor Consistency During Processing: Keep an eye on the consistency of your dessert during the processing cycle. If it looks too soft or hard, you may need to adjust the processing time in future batches.

14 Let the Mixture Rest Before Serving: After processing, let the dessert sit for a few minutes before serving. This settles the texture, especially for creamier desserts like ice cream or gelato.

15 Maintain Your Ninja CREAMi: Regular maintenance, such as checking the blades for sharpness and ensuring the motor base is clean, can prolong the life of your Ninja CREAMi and ensure it operates efficiently.

16 Pre-Mix Liquid Ingredients: For a smoother texture, pre-mix all liquid ingredients thoroughly before adding them to the CREAMi Pints. This prevents uneven freezing and chunky textures.

17 Use High-Quality Ingredients: The quality of the ingredients can significantly affect your dessert's outcome. Using high-quality, fresh ingredients will produce better-tasting and more satisfying desserts.

18 Adjust Recipes to Taste: Don't hesitate to adjust recipes according to your personal preference. Add more or less sugar, flavor extracts, or other ingredients to suit your taste.

19 Experiment with Dairy-Free Bases: For those who are lactose intolerant or following a vegan diet, experimenting with dairy-free milk alternatives like almond milk, coconut milk, or cashew milk can yield delicious results.

17 Chill Serving Dishes: For an extra touch, chill your serving bowls or glasses before dishing out your frozen dessert. This keeps it cold and creamy for longer while serving.

18 Be Mindful of Alcohol Content: If you're making adult-only frozen treats with alcohol, remember that too much alcohol can prevent the mixture from freezing correctly.

19 Freeze Decorative Elements: If you use fruits or edible flowers as a garnish, consider freezing them beforehand. This adds a nice touch to your presentation without melting the dessert.

By keeping these tips and tricks in mind, you can enhance your dessert-making experience with the Ninja CREAMi and delight in the endless possibilities of homemade frozen treats.

How to Use This Book

This chapter is your compass for navigating through the rich array of recipes contained within this book. Our goal is to help you effortlessly find and create the perfect dessert for any occasion, mood, or dietary preference.

Exploring the Variety

We've organized this book by the specific functions of the Ninja CREAMi, allowing you to quickly find the type of dessert you wish to make, from creamy ice creams and rich gelatos to vibrant sorbets, filling milkshakes, and nutritious smoothie bowls. While you may already be familiar with the capabilities of each function, we suggest exploring all sections to discover the full potential of your Ninja CREAMi. Diving into different functions might surprise you with new favorites.

Skill Level Indications

To accommodate all levels of culinary expertise, recipes are categorized as Beginner, Intermediate, and Advanced. These designations reflect the preparation complexity, ingredient sophistication, and precision needed. Whether you're aiming for a simple yet delightful treat or a challenging dessert masterpiece, you'll find recipes that match your current skill level and ambition.

Matched to Every Occasion

Each recipe comes with suggestions for ideal occasions, from casual evenings to festive gatherings. These recommendations are meant to inspire you to select the perfect dessert, enhancing any event from a serene night into an exuberant outdoor celebration with friends and family.

Quick Selection with Tags

To streamline your recipe selection process, we've included tags for flavor profiles (like fruity or chocolaty), alcohol content for adult desserts, and dietary preferences (such as vegan or gluten-free). These tags make it easy to pick a recipe that fits your preferences or dietary needs, ensuring that the delights you create can be enjoyed by all.

Beginning Your Culinary Exploration

With this cookbook, you embark on a culinary exploration that promises delightful discoveries with each recipe you try. The real magic of the Ninja CREAMi is not just its technological capabilities but the creative possibilities it unlocks. As you familiarize yourself with the diverse recipes and the functionalities of your Ninja CREAMi, we hope you're inspired to experiment, personalize, and perhaps even devise your own unique frozen creations. Here's to the culinary discoveries that lie ahead in your kitchen. May they bring as much joy in making as they do in tasting.

Cranberry Cheesecake Lite Ice Cream

Flavor profile: Creamy with a tangy cranberry twist.

| ❄ Freeze time **24 hours** | 🍲 Prep time **15 minutes** | ⏰ Function time **2 minutes** | ⏱ Servings **4** | 🔥 Calories **280** | Complexity **Beginner** |

Tags: Creamy, Tangy, Sweet, Vegetarian, Lite

Ninja CREAMi function: Ice Cream, Mix-In

Tools needed: Blender, mixing bowl, measuring cups, measuring spoons

Ingredients:

- 1 cup fresh cranberries
- 2 cups low-fat cream cheese, softened
- 1 cup low-fat Greek yogurt
- 3/4 cup granulated sugar
- 1 teaspoon vanilla extract
- 1/2 cup water

Directions:

1. In a small saucepan, combine cranberries and water. Cook over medium heat until the cranberries have popped and formed a thick sauce, about 5-7 minutes. Allow to cool completely.
2. In a blender, blend the cooled cranberry sauce, cream cheese, Greek yogurt, sugar, and vanilla extract until smooth.
3. Pour the mixture into a CREAMi Pint and seal with the Outer Bowl and Lid. Freeze until solid, typically for 24 hours.
4. Once frozen, install the Creamerizer Paddle to the Motor Base and attach the frozen pint. Use the Lid to secure it.
5. Select the "Lite Ice Cream" function on the Control Panel and start the process. Let the Ninja CREAMi churn the mixture until it achieves a smooth, creamy consistency.
6. Serve the Cranberry Cheesecake Lite Ice Cream immediately for a soft serve texture, or transfer to an airtight container and freeze for an additional 1-2 hours for a firmer texture.

Nutritional Information (per serving): Protein: 8g | Carbohydrates: 40g | Sodium: 300mg | Potassium: 200mg | Sugar: 35g

Gingerbread Cookie Delight Ice Cream

Flavor profile: Richly spiced with the warming tastes of ginger and cinnamon.

| ❄️ Freeze time **24 hours** | Prep time **10 minutes** | Function time **2 minutes** | Servings **4** | Calories **315** | Complexity **Beginner** |

Tags: Creamy, Spiced, Sweet, Kid Friendly   **Ninja CREAMi function:** Ice Cream, Mix-In

Tools needed: Mixing bowl, whisk, measuring cups, measuring spoons

Ingredients:

- 2 cups whole milk
- 1 cup heavy cream
- 1/2 cup granulated sugar
- 1 teaspoon ground ginger
- 1 teaspoon ground cinnamon
- 3 medium-sized gingerbread cookies, crumbled

Directions:

1. In a mixing bowl, combine whole milk, heavy cream, and granulated sugar. Whisk together until the sugar has completely dissolved.
2. Stir in the ground ginger and cinnamon until well mixed.
3. Transfer the mixture into a CREAMi Pint and seal the Outer Bowl and Lid. Freeze the mixture in your freezer until solid, typically for 24 hours.
4. Once frozen, install the Creamerizer Paddle to the Motor Base, and insert the frozen pint into the Outer Bowl. Attach the Lid and select the "Ice Cream" function on the Control Panel to churn the ice cream.
5. After the ice cream cycle completes, add the crumbled gingerbread cookies to the pint. Replace the Lid and select the "Mix-In" function to evenly distribute the cookie pieces throughout the ice cream.
6. Serve immediately for a soft-serve texture, or transfer the ice cream to an airtight container and freeze for an additional 1-2 hours for a firmer consistency.

Nutritional Information (per serving): Protein: 4g | Carbohydrates: 34g | Sodium: 105mg | Potassium: 161mg | Sugar: 29g

Peppermint Mocha Milkshake

Flavor profile: A creamy blend of chocolate and peppermint, with a festive touch.

| ❄️ Freeze time **24 hours** | Prep time **10 minutes** | Function time **1 minute** | Servings **4** | Calories **280** | Complexity **Beginner** |

Tags: Refreshing, Creamy, Sweet, Kid Friendly, Vegetarian   **Ninja CREAMi function:** Milkshake

Tools needed: Refreshing, Creamy, Sweet, Kid Friendly, Vegetarian

Ingredients:

- 3 cups vanilla ice cream
- 1 cup cold brew coffee
- 1/2 cup milk
- 1/4 cup chocolate syrup
- 2 tablespoons crushed peppermint candies, plus extra for garnish

Directions:

1. In a blender, combine vanilla ice cream, cold brew coffee, milk, and chocolate syrup. Blend until smooth.
2. Add crushed peppermint candies to the blender and pulse a few times to mix them into the shake lightly.
3. Pour the mixture into a CREAMi Pint and secure the Outer Bowl and Lid. Attach the pint to the Motor Base with the Creamerizer Paddle installed.
4. Select the "Milkshake" function on the Control Panel and start the process to churn the mixture until it reaches a smooth, creamy milkshake consistency.
5. Pour the milkshake into glasses and garnish with additional crushed peppermint candies.
6. Serve immediately and enjoy a festive, cooling treat.

Nutritional Information (per serving): Protein: 4g | Carbohydrates: 44g | Sodium: 170mg | Potassium: 263mg | Sugar: 38g

Christmas Pudding Sorbet

Flavor profile: Creamy with a tangy cranberry twist.

❄️ Freeze time **24 hours**	⏲️ Prep time **30 minutes**	⏰ Function time **2 minutes**	⏱️ Servings **4**	🔥 Calories **180**	Complexity **Intermediate**

Tags: Fruity, Spiced, Refreshing, Vegetarian, Dairy Free, Gluten Free, Vegan   **Ninja CREAMi function:** Sorbet

Tools needed: Saucepan, blender, mixing bowl, measuring cups, measuring spoons, fine mesh sieve

Ingredients:

- 1 cup dried mixed fruit (raisins, currants, and sultanas)
- 1 small apple, peeled, cored, and finely chopped
- Zest and juice of 1 orange
- 1/2 cup dark brown sugar
- 1 cup water
- 1 teaspoon mixed spice (cinnamon, nutmeg, and cloves)
- 1 teaspoon vanilla extract
- 1 tablespoon dark rum (optional)

Directions:

1. In a saucepan, combine dried fruit, chopped apple, orange zest, orange juice, dark brown sugar, and water. Bring to a boil, then reduce heat and simmer for 15-20 minutes until the fruit is soft and the mixture has thickened slightly.
2. Remove from heat and allow to cool slightly. Add the mixed spice, vanilla extract, and dark rum (if using), and blend the mixture until smooth using a blender.
3. Strain the fruit mixture through a fine mesh sieve into a mixing bowl, pressing down with a spoon to extract as much liquid as possible.
4. Pour the strained mixture into a CREAMi Pint and secure with the Outer Bowl and Lid. Freeze the mixture for 24 hours until solid.
5. Once frozen, install the Creamerizer Paddle to the Motor Base and insert the frozen pint into the Outer Bowl. Attach the Lid.
6. Select the "Sorbet" function on the Control Panel and start the process. Allow the Ninja CREAMi to churn the frozen mixture until it achieves a smooth, sorbet consistency.
7. Serve the Christmas Pudding Sorbet immediately, or transfer to an airtight container and store in the freezer until ready to serve.

Nutritional Information (per serving): Protein: 1g | Carbohydrates: 44g | Sodium: 20mg | Potassium: 210mg | Sugar: 38g

Festive Eggnog Ice Cream

Flavor profile: Creamy and rich with a distinctive eggnog spice.

❄ Freeze time **24 hours**	Prep time **10 minutes**	Function time **2 minutes**	Servings **4**	Calories **420**	Complexity **Beginner**

Tags: Creamy, Spiced, Sweet, Kid Friendly, Vegetarian *Ninja CREAMi function:* Ice Cream

Tools needed: Mixing bowl, whisk, measuring cups, measuring spoons

Ingredients:

- 2 cups prepared eggnog
- 1 cup heavy cream
- 1/2 cup granulated sugar
- 1 teaspoon ground nutmeg
- 1 teaspoon vanilla extract

Directions:

1. In a mixing bowl, whisk together prepared eggnog, heavy cream, granulated sugar, ground nutmeg, and vanilla extract until the sugar is completely dissolved.
2. Pour the mixture into a CREAMi Pint and secure the Outer Bowl and Lid. Place the pint in your freezer and freeze until solid, typically for 24 hours.
3. Once frozen, attach the Creamerizer Paddle to the Motor Base, insert the frozen pint into the Outer Bowl, and secure the Lid.
4. Select the "Ice Cream" function on the Control Panel and start the process. Let the Ninja CREAMi churn the mixture until it reaches a smooth and creamy consistency.
5. Serve the Festive Eggnog Ice Cream immediately for a soft-serve texture, or transfer to an airtight container and freeze for an additional 1-2 hours for a firmer texture.

Nutritional Information (per serving): Protein: 4g | Carbohydrates: 33g | Sodium: 95mg | Potassium: 180mg | Sugar: 31g

---

Hot Chocolate Marshmallow Ice Cream

Flavor profile: Rich chocolatey ice cream with soft, sweet marshmallow pieces.

❄ Freeze time **24 hours**	Prep time **15 minutes**	Function time **2 minutes**	Servings **4**	Calories **410**	Complexity **Beginner**

Tags: Creamy, Sweet, Kid Friendly *Ninja CREAMi function:* Ice Cream, Mix-In

Tools needed: Saucepan, mixing bowl, whisk, measuring cups, measuring spoons

Ingredients:

- 2 cups heavy cream
- 1 cup whole milk
- 1/2 cup granulated sugar
- 1/3 cup cocoa powder
- 1 cup mini marshmallows

Directions:

1. In a saucepan over medium heat, combine heavy cream, whole milk, granulated sugar, and cocoa powder. Whisk continuously until the mixture is smooth and the sugar and cocoa are completely dissolved. Do not boil. Remove from heat and allow to cool to room temperature.
2. Once cooled, pour the chocolate mixture into a CREAMi Pint and secure with the Outer Bowl and Lid. Freeze for 24 hours until solid.
3. Attach the Creamerizer Paddle to the Motor Base, insert the frozen pint into the Outer Bowl, and secure the Lid.
4. Select the "Ice Cream" function on the Control Panel and start the process. Allow the Ninja CREAMi to churn the mixture until it achieves a smooth ice cream consistency.
5. After the ice cream cycle completes, open the lid and add the mini marshmallows. Close the lid and select the "Mix-In" function to evenly incorporate the marshmallows throughout the ice cream.
6. Serve the Hot Chocolate Marshmallow Ice Cream immediately for a soft serve texture, or transfer to an airtight container and freeze for an additional 1-2 hours for a firmer consistency.

Nutritional Information (per serving): Protein: 4g | Carbohydrates: 36g | Sodium: 70mg | Potassium: 200mg | Sugar: 31g

Spiced Pear Cider Sorbet

Flavor profile: Fresh, tangy pear with a subtle hint of warming spices.

❄ Freeze time **24 hours**	🍲 Prep time **20 minutes**	⏰ Function time **2 minutes**	⏱ Servings **4**	🔥 Calories **180**	Complexity **Intermediate**

Tags: Refreshing, Spiced, Sweet, Tangy, Vegan, Gluten Free, Dairy Free, Fruity   ***Ninja CREAMi function:*** Sorbet
Tools needed: Saucepan, blender, mixing bowl, fine mesh strainer, measuring cups, measuring spoons

Ingredients:

- 4 ripe pears, peeled, cored, and chopped
- 2 cups water
- 3/4 cup granulated sugar
- Juice of 1 lemon
- 1 cinnamon stick
- 3 cloves
- 1 star anise

Directions:

1. In a saucepan, combine chopped pears, water, sugar, lemon juice, cinnamon stick, cloves, and star anise. Bring to a boil, then reduce heat and simmer for 10-15 minutes until the pears are very soft.
2. Remove from heat and discard the cinnamon stick, cloves, and star anise.
3. Transfer the mixture to a blender and puree until smooth.
4. Strain the pear puree through a fine mesh strainer into a mixing bowl, pressing the solids to extract as much liquid as possible.
5. Pour the strained pear mixture into a CREAMi Pint and secure with the Outer Bowl and Lid. Freeze for 24 hours until solid.
6. Once frozen, install the Creamerizer Paddle to the Motor Base and insert the frozen pint into the Outer Bowl. Secure the Lid.
7. Select the "Sorbet" function on the Control Panel and start the process. Allow the Ninja CREAMi to churn the mixture until it achieves a smooth, sorbet consistency.
8. Serve the Spiced Pear Cider Sorbet immediately for the best texture or transfer to an airtight container and store in the freezer if not serving immediately.

Nutritional Information (per serving): Protein: 0.5g | Carbohydrates: 46g | Sodium: 5mg | Potassium: 120mg | Sugar: 42g

Winter Spice Apple Gelato

Flavor profile: Rich apple with a complex melody of winter spices.

❄ Freeze time **24 hours**	Prep time **20 minutes**	Function time **2 minutes**	Servings **4**	Calories **230**	Complexity **Intermediate**

Tags: Refreshing, Creamy, Spiced, Sweet, Fruity, Vegetarian   **Ninja CREAMi function:** Gelato

Tools needed: Saucepan, blender, mixing bowl, sieve, spatula, measuring cups, measuring spoons

Ingredients:

- 2 large apples, peeled, cored, and chopped
- 1 cup whole milk
- 1/2 cup heavy cream
- 1/2 cup granulated sugar
- 1 teaspoon ground cinnamon
- 1/4 teaspoon ground nutmeg

Directions:

1. In a saucepan, cook the chopped apples with a splash of water over medium heat until they are tender and almost falling apart, about 10-15 minutes. Allow them to cool slightly.
2. Transfer the cooked apples to a blender and blend until very smooth. Pass the apple puree through a sieve to ensure a fine texture, pressing with the back of a spoon or a spatula to extract as much fluid as possible.
3. In a mixing bowl, whisk together the apple puree, whole milk, heavy cream, granulated sugar, cinnamon, and nutmeg until the sugar is completely dissolved and the mixture is homogeneous.
4. Pour the smooth mixture into a CREAMi Pint, ensuring it is sealed well with the Outer Bowl and Lid. Freeze the pint for at least 24 hours until the mixture is solid. Once the base is frozen, assemble the Creamerizer Paddle with the Motor Base, and place the frozen pint secured with the Outer Bowl and Lid.
5. Select the "Gelato" function on the Control Panel. Start the Ninja CREAMi to churn the frozen base until it reaches a smooth and dense gelato consistency, typically taking about 2 minutes.
6. Serve the gelato immediately if you prefer a softer consistency, or transfer it to an airtight container and store in the freezer for 1-2 hours for a firmer texture that is ideal for scooping.

Nutritional Information (per serving): Protein: 2g | Carbohydrates: 37g | Sodium: 45mg | Potassium: 120mg | Sugar: 34g

---

Candy Cane Crunch Ice Cream

Flavor profile: Creamy vanilla with refreshing bursts of peppermint candy.

❄ Freeze time **24 hours**	Prep time **10 minutes**	Function time **2 minutes**	Servings **4**	Calories **440**	Complexity **Beginner**

Tags: Creamy, Sweet, Kid Friendly, Vegetarian   **Ninja CREAMi function:** Ice Cream, Mix-In

Tools needed: Mixing bowl, spoon, measuring cups, measuring spoons

Ingredients:

- 2 cups heavy cream
- 1 cup whole milk
- 3/4 cup granulated sugar
- 1 teaspoon vanilla extract
- 1/2 cup crushed candy canes

Directions:

1. In a mixing bowl, combine heavy cream, whole milk, granulated sugar, and vanilla extract. Stir until the sugar is completely dissolved.
2. Pour the mixture into a CREAMi Pint and secure the Outer Bowl and Lid. Freeze the pint for 24 hours until solid.
3. Once frozen, attach the Creamerizer Paddle to the Motor Base and insert the frozen pint into the Outer Bowl. Secure the Lid.
4. Select the "Ice Cream" function on the Control Panel and start the process. Allow the Ninja CREAMi to churn the mixture until it reaches a smooth and creamy ice cream consistency.
5. After the ice cream cycle completes, open the lid and add the crushed candy canes. Close the lid and select the "Mix-In" function to evenly distribute the candy pieces throughout the ice cream.
6. Serve the Candy Cane Crunch Ice Cream immediately for a soft serve texture, or transfer to an airtight container and freeze for an additional 1-2 hours for a firmer consistency.

Nutritional Information (per serving): Protein: 3g | Carbohydrates: 44g | Sodium: 70mg | Potassium: 130mg | Sugar: 40g

Pistachio & Cherry Gelato

Flavor profile: Nutty pistachios perfectly balanced with sweet and tart cherries.

| ❄️ Freeze time **24 hours** | 🍲 Prep time **20 minutes** | ⏰ Function time **2 minutes** | 🕐 Servings **4** | 🔥 Calories **390** | 〰️ Complexity **Intermediate** |

Tags: Creamy, Nutty, Fruity, Sweet, Vegetarian   ***Ninja CREAMi function:*** Gelato

Tools needed: Food processor, mixing bowl, measuring cups, measuring spoons, spatula

Ingredients:

- 1 cup unsalted pistachios, shelled
- 1 cup cherries, pitted and halved (fresh or frozen)
- 2 cups whole milk
- 1 cup heavy cream
- 3/4 cup granulated sugar
- 1 teaspoon almond extract

Directions:

1. In a food processor, grind the pistachios into a fine powder. Set aside a small amount for garnish if desired.
2. In a mixing bowl, combine the ground pistachios, whole milk, heavy cream, granulated sugar, and almond extract. Stir well until the sugar is completely dissolved.
3. Add the halved cherries to the mixture and stir gently to incorporate.
4. Pour the mixture into a CREAMi Pint and secure with the Outer Bowl and Lid. Freeze the pint for 24 hours until solid.
5. Once frozen, attach the Creamerizer Paddle to the Motor Base, and place the frozen pint into the Outer Bowl. Secure the Lid.
6. Select the "Gelato" function on the Control Panel and start the process. Let the Ninja CREAMi churn the mixture until it achieves a smooth and dense gelato consistency.
7. Serve the Pistachio & Cherry Gelato immediately for the best texture, or transfer to an airtight container and freeze for an additional 1-2 hours if a firmer consistency is desired. Garnish with reserved ground pistachios before serving.

Nutritional Information (per serving): Protein: 7g | Carbohydrates: 36g | Sodium: 55mg | Potassium: 330mg | Sugar: 33g

Yuletide Orange Chocolate Ice Cream

Flavor profile: Luxuriously rich chocolate with a refreshing hint of citrus.

❄ Freeze time **24 hours**	⏲ Prep time **15 minutes**	🕐 Function time **2 minutes**	🍕 Servings **4**	🔥 Calories **430**	⬤— Complexity **Beginner**

Tags: Creamy, Sweet, Fruity, Vegetarian, Kid Friendly   ***Ninja CREAMi function:*** Ice Cream

Tools needed: Mixing bowl, zester, whisk, measuring cups, measuring spoons

Ingredients:

- 2 cups heavy cream
- 1 cup whole milk
- 3/4 cup granulated sugar
- 1/3 cup unsweetened cocoa powder
- Zest of 1 large orange

Directions:

1. In a mixing bowl, whisk together heavy cream, whole milk, granulated sugar, and cocoa powder until the sugar and cocoa are completely dissolved. Stir in the zest of one large orange to infuse the mixture with citrus flavor.
2. Pour the mixture into a CREAMi Pint and secure with the Outer Bowl and Lid. Place the pint in the freezer and freeze until solid, typically for 24 hours. Once frozen, attach the Creamerizer Paddle to the Motor Base, and place the frozen pint into the Outer Bowl. Secure the Lid.
3. Select the "Ice Cream" function on the Control Panel and start the process. Let the Ninja CREAMi churn the mixture until it reaches a smooth and creamy ice cream consistency.
4. Serve the Yuletide Orange Chocolate Ice Cream immediately for a soft serve texture, or transfer to an airtight container and freeze for an additional 1-2 hours for a firmer texture.

Nutritional Information (per serving): Protein: 4g | Carbohydrates: 39g | Sodium: 60mg | Potassium: 210mg | Sugar: 35g

Mince Pie Lite Ice Cream

Flavor profile: Richly spiced with fruits and a hint of brandy, encapsulating the essence of mince pie.

❄ Freeze time **24 hours**	⏲ Prep time **15 minutes**	🕐 Function time **2 minutes**	🍕 Servings **4**	🔥 Calories **210**	⬤— Complexity **Intermediate**

Tags: Lite, Creamy, Spiced, Sweet, Fruity, Vegetarian   ***Ninja CREAMi function:*** Lite Ice Cream

Tools needed: Mixing bowl, spatula, measuring cups, measuring spoons

Ingredients:

- 1 cup prepared mince(store-bought or homemade)
- 1 cup low-fat milk
- 1/2 cup heavy cream
- 1/4 cup granulated sugar
- 2 tablespoons brandy (optional)
- 1 teaspoon vanilla extract
- 1/2 teaspoon ground cinnamon

Directions:

1. In a mixing bowl, combine the mince, low-fat milk, heavy cream, granulated sugar, brandy (if using), vanilla extract, and ground cinnamon. Stir thoroughly until the sugar is dissolved and the mixture is well combined.
2. Pour the mixture into a CREAMi Pint and secure with the Outer Bowl and Lid. Freeze the pint for 24 hours until solid.
3. Once frozen, attach the Creamerizer Paddle to the Motor Base, and place the frozen pint into the Outer Bowl. Secure the Lid.
4. Select the "Lite Ice Cream" function on the Control Panel and start the process. Let the Ninja CREAMi churn the mixture until it reaches a smooth, creamy consistency typical of lite ice cream.
5. Serve the Mince Pie Lite Ice Cream immediately for a soft serve texture, or transfer to an airtight container and freeze for an additional 1-2 hours for a firmer texture.

Nutritional Information (per serving): Protein: 3g | Carbohydrates: 35g | Sodium: 55mg | Potassium: 90mg | Sugar: 30g

Mulled Wine Sorbet

Flavor profile: Aromatic and spiced with a deep red wine base, perfect for a festive palate cleanser.

| ❄️ Freeze time **24 hours** | 🍲 Prep time **15 minutes** | ⏰ Function time **2 minutes** | ⏱️ Servings **4** | 🔥 Calories **180** | Complexity **Intermediate** |

Tags: Refreshing, Spiced, Sweet, Tangy, Adults Only, Gluten Free, Vegan, Dairy Free

Ninja CREAMi function: Sorbet

Tools needed: Saucepan, measuring cups, measuring spoons, fine mesh sieve

Ingredients:

- 2 cups red wine (preferably a fruity variety like Merlot or Zinfandel)
- 1/2 cup water
- 3/4 cup granulated sugar
- Peel of 1 orange
- 2 cinnamon sticks
- 4 cloves
- 1 star anise

Directions:

1. In a saucepan, combine red wine, water, granulated sugar, orange peel, cinnamon sticks, cloves, and star anise. Heat over medium heat, stirring until the sugar dissolves and the mixture just reaches a simmer—do not allow to boil. Remove from heat and let steep for 10 minutes to infuse the spices.
2. Strain the mulled wine mixture through a fine mesh sieve into a bowl, removing the spices and orange peel.
3. Allow the mixture to cool to room temperature, then pour into a CREAMi Pint and secure with the Outer Bowl and Lid. Freeze for 24 hours until solid.
4. Once frozen, attach the Creamerizer Paddle to the Motor Base, and place the frozen pint into the Outer Bowl. Secure the Lid.
5. Select the "Sorbet" function on the Control Panel and start the process. Let the Ninja CREAMi churn the mixture until it reaches a smooth, sorbet consistency.
6. Serve the Mulled Wine Sorbet immediately for the best texture or transfer to an airtight container and store in the freezer if not serving immediately.

Nutritional Information (per serving): Protein: 0g | Carbohydrates: 26g | Sodium: 5mg | Potassium: 100mg | Sugar: 24g

Toffee Nut Latte Milkshake

Flavor profile: Creamy and sweet with a robust espresso and nutty toffee twist.

❄️ Freeze time	🍲 Prep time	⏰ Function time	🕐 Servings	🔥 Calories	⎯○ Complexity
24 hours	**10 minutes**	**1 minutes**	**4**	**340**	**Beginner**

Tags: Creamy, Sweet, Nutty, Kid Friendly, Vegetarian   **Ninja CREAMi function:** Milkshake

Tools needed: Blender, measuring cups, measuring spoons

Ingredients:

- 3 cups vanilla ice cream
- 1 cup cold espresso or strong brewed coffee
- 1/2 cup milk
- 1/4 cup toffee syrup
- Whipped cream and crushed toffee nuts for garnish

Directions:

1. Place vanilla ice cream, cold espresso, milk, and toffee syrup into a blender. Blend until smooth and well combined.
2. Pour the mixture into a CREAMi Pint and secure with the Outer Bowl and Lid. Attach the pint to the Motor Base with the Creamerizer Paddle installed.
3. Select the "Milkshake" function on the Control Panel and start the process. Let the Ninja CREAMi churn the mixture until it reaches a creamy, smooth milkshake consistency.
4. Pour the milkshake into serving glasses, top with whipped cream, and sprinkle with crushed toffee nuts for garnish.
5. Serve immediately and enjoy this festive and flavorful treat.

Nutritional Information (per serving): Protein: 5g | Carbohydrates: 45g | Sodium: 120mg | Potassium: 250mg | Sugar: 40g

---

Figgy Pudding Ice Cream

Flavor profile: Rich and spiced with a deep fig and dried fruit essence.

❄️ Freeze time	🍲 Prep time	⏰ Function time	🕐 Servings	🔥 Calories	⎯○ Complexity
24 hours	**15 minutes**	**2 minutes**	**4**	**580**	**Intermediate**

Tags: Creamy, Spiced, Sweet, Fruity, Vegetarian   **Ninja CREAMi function:** Ice Cream

Tools needed: Mixing bowl, saucepan, wooden spoon, measuring cups, measuring spoons

Ingredients:

- 1 cup dried figs, chopped
- 1/2 cup mixed dried fruit (raisins, sultanas, currants)
- 1/4 cup dark rum or brandy
- 2 cups heavy cream
- 1 cup whole milk
- 3/4 cup brown sugar
- 1 teaspoon ground cinnamon
- 1/4 teaspoon ground nutmeg

Directions:

1. In a small saucepan, combine chopped figs, mixed dried fruit, and rum or brandy. Simmer over low heat for 5 minutes until the fruit is plump and softened. Set aside to cool.
2. In a mixing bowl, whisk together heavy cream, whole milk, brown sugar, ground cinnamon, and ground nutmeg until the sugar is dissolved.
3. Stir the cooled fruit mixture into the cream mixture, ensuring it's well combined. Pour the mixture into a CREAMi Pint and secure with the Outer Bowl and Lid. Freeze the pint for 24 hours until solid.
4. Once frozen, attach the Creamerizer Paddle to the Motor Base, and place the frozen pint into the Outer Bowl. Secure the Lid.
5. Select the "Ice Cream" function on the Control Panel and start the process. Let the Ninja CREAMi churn the mixture until it achieves a smooth and creamy ice cream consistency.
6. Serve the Figgy Pudding Ice Cream immediately for a soft serve texture, or transfer to an airtight container and freeze for an additional 1-2 hours for a firmer texture.

Nutritional Information (per serving): Protein: 5g | Carbohydrates: 77g | Sodium: 85mg | Potassium: 430mg | Sugar: 66g

Cinnamon Roll Lite Ice Cream

Flavor profile: Sweet and warmly spiced with a swirl of cinnamon and a hint of vanilla.

❄ Freeze time **24 hours**	Prep time **15 minutes**	⏰ Function time **2 minutes**	Servings **4**	Calories **180**	Complexity **Beginner**

Tags: Lite, Creamy, Spiced, Sweet, Kid Friendly

Ninja CREAMi function: Lite Ice Cream

Tools needed: Mixing bowl, whisk, measuring cups, measuring spoons

Ingredients:

- 2 cups low-fat milk
- 1 cup light cream
- 1/2 cup brown sugar
- 2 teaspoons ground cinnamon
- 1 teaspoon vanilla extract
- Pinch of salt

Directions:

1. In a mixing bowl, combine low-fat milk, light cream, brown sugar, ground cinnamon, vanilla extract, and a pinch of salt. Whisk together until the sugar is completely dissolved and the mixture is smooth.
2. Pour the mixture into a CREAMi Pint and secure with the Outer Bowl and Lid. Place the pint in the freezer and freeze until solid, typically for 24 hours.
3. Once frozen, attach the Creamerizer Paddle to the Motor Base, and place the frozen pint into the Outer Bowl. Secure the Lid.
4. Select the "Lite Ice Cream" function on the Control Panel and start the process. Allow the Ninja CREAMi to churn the mixture until it reaches a smooth and creamy lite ice cream consistency.
5. Serve the Cinnamon Roll Lite Ice Cream immediately for a soft serve texture, or transfer to an airtight container and freeze for an additional 1-2 hours for a firmer texture.

Nutritional Information (per serving): Protein: 4g | Carbohydrates: 28g | Sodium: 100mg | Potassium: 200mg | Sugar: 25g

Pumpkin Spice Smoothie Bowl

Flavor profile: A creamy blend of pumpkin and classic fall spices topped with a crunchy mix of nuts and seeds.

❄️ Freeze time **24 hours**	Prep time **10 minutes**	Function time **1 minutes**	Servings **2**	Calories **280**	Complexity **Beginner**

Tags: Vegetarian, Kid Friendly, Creamy, Spiced, Sweet, Nutty, Fruity   *Ninja CREAMi function:* Smoothie Bowl

Tools needed: Blender, measuring cups, measuring spoons, bowls for serving

Ingredients:

- 1 cup pumpkin puree (canned or fresh)
- 1 frozen banana
- 1/2 cup Greek yogurt
- 1/2 cup milk (dairy or non-dairy)
- 2 tablespoons maple syrup
- 1 teaspoon pumpkin pie spice
- Toppings: granola, pumpkin seeds, sliced banana, a drizzle of honey

Directions:

1. In a blender, combine the pumpkin puree, frozen banana, Greek yogurt, milk, maple syrup, and pumpkin pie spice. Blend until the mixture is smooth and creamy.
2. Pour the mixture into a CREAMi Pint and secure with the Outer Bowl and Lid. Attach the pint to the Motor Base with the Creamerizer Paddle installed.
3. Select the "Smoothie Bowl" function on the Control Panel and start the process. Allow the Ninja CREAMi to churn the mixture until it reaches a thick, smooth consistency suitable for a smoothie bowl.
4. Spoon the smoothie mixture into bowls and top with granola, pumpkin seeds, sliced banana, and a drizzle of honey. Serve immediately, and enjoy this nourishing and festive breakfast or snack.

Nutritional Information (per serving): Protein: 8g | Carbohydrates: 53g | Sodium: 60mg | Potassium: 500mg | Sugar: 35g

Spiced Orange and Cranberry Ripple Ice Cream

Flavor profile: Citrusy and tart with a spiced ripple, blending the freshness of orange with the zing of cranberries.

❄️ Freeze time **24 hours**	Prep time **20 minutes**	Function time **2 minutes**	Servings **4**	Calories **400**	Complexity **Intermediate**

Tags: Creamy, Sweet, Tangy, Fruity, Vegetarian   *Ninja CREAMi function:* Ice Cream

Tools needed: Saucepan, blender, mixing bowl, whisk, measuring cups, measuring spoons

Ingredients:

- 2 cups heavy cream
- 1 cup whole milk
- 3/4 cup granulated sugar
- Zest of 1 orange
- 1/2 cup cranberry sauce (homemade or store-bought)
- 1 teaspoon vanilla extract
- 1/2 teaspoon ground cinnamon

Directions:

1. In a saucepan, combine heavy cream, whole milk, granulated sugar, orange zest, vanilla extract, and ground cinnamon. Heat over medium heat, stirring frequently until the sugar dissolves and the mixture is just beginning to simmer. Remove from heat and allow to cool to room temperature, then chill in the refrigerator.
2. Once chilled, pour the mixture into a CREAMi Pint and secure with the Outer Bowl and Lid. Freeze for 24 hours until solid.
3. After freezing, attach the Creamerizer Paddle to the Motor Base, and place the frozen pint into the Outer Bowl. Secure the Lid.
4. Select the "Ice Cream" function on the Control Panel and start the process. Let the Ninja CREAMi churn the mixture until it reaches a smooth and creamy texture.
5. Midway through churning, add the cranberry sauce in dollops over the soft ice cream. Resume churning to create a ripple effect with the cranberry sauce.
6. Serve the Spiced Orange and Cranberry Ripple Ice Cream immediately for a soft serve texture, or transfer to an airtight container and freeze for an additional 1-2 hours for a firmer consistency.

Nutritional Information (per serving): Protein: 3g | Carbohydrates: 30g | Sodium: 50mg | Potassium: 100mg | Sugar: 29g

Roasted Chestnut Gelato

Flavor profile: Nutty and creamy with a hint of natural sweetness from roasted chestnuts.

❄ Freeze time **24 hours**	🍲 Prep time **20 minutes**	🕐 Function time **2 minutes**	⏲ Servings **4**	🔥 Calories **390**	Complexity **Intermediate**

Tags: Creamy, Nutty, Sweet, Vegetarian   **Ninja CREAMi function:** Gelato

Tools needed: Oven, food processor, saucepan, mixing bowl, measuring cups, measuring spoons

Ingredients:

- 1 cup roasted chestnuts, peeled
- 2 cups whole milk
- 1 cup heavy cream
- 2/3 cup granulated sugar
- 1 teaspoon vanilla extract
- Pinch of salt

Directions:

1. Preheat your oven to 400°F (200°C). Spread chestnuts on a baking sheet and roast for about 15-20 minutes, or until they are fragrant and slightly browned. Allow them to cool, then peel and chop coarsely.
2. In a food processor, pulse the roasted chestnuts until finely ground.
3. In a saucepan over medium heat, combine ground chestnuts, whole milk, heavy cream, granulated sugar, and a pinch of salt. Cook, stirring frequently, until the sugar is dissolved and the mixture is heated through but not boiling.
4. Remove from heat and stir in vanilla extract. Allow the mixture to cool completely, then refrigerate until chilled.
5. Pour the chilled mixture into a CREAMi Pint and secure with the Outer Bowl and Lid. Freeze for 24 hours until solid.
6. Once frozen, attach the Creamerizer Paddle to the Motor Base, and place the frozen pint into the Outer Bowl. Secure the Lid.
7. Select the "Gelato" function on the Control Panel and start the process. Let the Ninja CREAMi churn the mixture until it achieves a smooth and dense gelato consistency.
8. Serve the Roasted Chestnut Gelato immediately for the best texture, or transfer to an airtight container and freeze for an additional 1-2 hours if a firmer consistency is desired.

Nutritional Information (per serving): Protein: 6g | Carbohydrates: 44g | Sodium: 80mg | Potassium: 250mg | Sugar: 38g

New Year's Eve Berry Sorbet

Flavor profile: Bright and tangy, bursting with a mix of sweet and tart berry flavors.

| ❄️ Freeze time **24 hours** | Prep time **10 minutes** | ⏰ Function time **2 minutes** | Servings **4** | Calories **180** | Complexity **Beginner** |

Tags: Refreshing, Sweet, Tangy, Fruity, Vegan, Gluten Free, Dairy Free

Ninja CREAMi function: Sorbet

Tools needed: Blender, mixing bowl, measuring cups, measuring spoons

Ingredients:

- 3 cups mixed berries (such as strawberries, raspberries, blueberries), fresh or frozen
- 1 cup water
- 3/4 cup granulated sugar
- Juice of 1 lemon

Directions:

1. If using fresh berries, wash and hull them. If using frozen berries, allow them to thaw slightly. In a blender, combine the mixed berries, water, granulated sugar, and lemon juice. Blend until smooth.
2. Pour the berry mixture through a fine mesh sieve into a mixing bowl to remove any seeds and pulp, pressing the solids with a spoon to extract as much liquid as possible. Pour the strained mixture into a CREAMi Pint and secure with the Outer Bowl and Lid. Place the pint in the freezer and freeze until solid, typically for 24 hours.
3. Once frozen, attach the Creamerizer Paddle to the Motor Base, and place the frozen pint into the Outer Bowl. Secure the Lid.
4. Select the "Sorbet" function on the Control Panel and start the process. Let the Ninja CREAMi churn the mixture until it reaches a smooth, sorbet consistency.
5. Serve the New Year's Eve Berry Sorbet immediately for the best texture, or transfer to an airtight container and store in the freezer if not serving immediately.

Nutritional Information (per serving): Protein: 1g | Carbohydrates: 46g | Sodium: 5mg | Potassium: 90mg | Sugar: 44g

Blood Orange & Vanilla Ice Cream

Flavor profile: Citrusy Blood Orange with Sweet Vanilla
Best for occasions: Summer Gatherings

❄ Freeze time **24 hours**	⏲ Prep time **20 minutes**	⏰ Function time **1,5 minutes**	⏱ Servings **4**	🔥 Calories **280**	Complexity **Beginner**

Tags: Refreshing, Creamy, Sweet, Fruity   **Ninja CREAMi function:** Ice Cream

Tools needed: Large bowl, whisk, measuring cups and spoons, CREAMI pint

Ingredients:

- 1 tablespoon cream cheese
- 1 cup heavy cream
- 1 cup whole milk
- 1/2 cup granulated sugar
- Juice and zest of 2 blood oranges
- 1 teaspoon vanilla extract

Directions:

1. Soften the cream cheese in the microwave for 10 seconds.
2. In a large mixing bowl, whisk together the softened cream cheese, heavy cream, whole milk, granulated sugar, blood orange juice and zest, vanilla extract, and a pinch of salt until smooth.
3. Pour the mixture into a Ninja CREAMi pint container.
4. Freeze the pint for 24 hours to ensure a solid freeze.
5. After freezing, insert the pint into the Ninja CREAMi.
6. Select the 'Ice Cream' function and process for 1.5 minutes.
7. Check the consistency after processing; use the 'Re-spin' cycle for a firmer texture if needed.
8. Serve immediately or store in the freezer in an airtight container.

Nutritional Information (per serving): Protein: 3g | Carbohydrates: 23g | Sodium: 80mg | Potassium: 150mg | Sugar: 22g

Basil & Lemon Zest Ice Cream

Flavor profile: perfect harmony of herbaceous notes and tangy lemon, offering a sophisticated and refreshing twist on traditional ice cream.
Best for occasions: Fancy Dinner Parties

| ❄️ Freeze time **24 hours** | 🍲 Prep time **15 minutes** | ⏰ Function time **1,5 minutes** | 🕐 Servings **4** | 🔥 Calories **300** | Complexity **Intermediate** |

Tags: Herbal, Refreshing, Creamy, Sweet   **Ninja CREAMi function:** Ice Cream

Tools needed: Large bowl, whisk, measuring cups and spoons, Ninja CREAMi pint

Ingredients:

- 1 tablespoon cream cheese
- 1 cup heavy cream
- 1 cup whole milk
- 1/2 cup granulated sugar
- Zest of 2 lemons
- 1/4 cup fresh basil leaves, finely chopped
- Pinch of salt

Directions:

1. Soften the cream cheese in the microwave for 10 seconds.
2. In a large bowl, whisk together the softened cream cheese, heavy cream, whole milk, granulated sugar, lemon zest, chopped basil, and a pinch of salt until smooth.
3. Pour the mixture into the Ninja CREAMi pint container.
4. Freeze the pint for 24 hours, ensuring a solid freeze.
5. Before inserting it into the Ninja CREAMi, remove the CREAMi Pint lid.
6. Place the frozen pint in the Ninja CREAMi.
7. Select the 'Ice Cream' function and process for 1.5 minutes.
8. Check the consistency after processing. If a firmer texture is desired, use the 'Re-spin' cycle.
9. Serve immediately or store in an airtight container in the freezer.

Nutritional Information (per serving): Protein: 3g | Carbohydrates: 24g | Sodium: 80mg | Potassium: 110mg | Sugar: 23g

---

Espresso Ice Cream

Flavor profile: Deep, bold espresso notes with a creamy backdrop, perfect for a rich and indulgent taste experience.
Best for occasions: Adults Only, Movie Night

| ❄️ Freeze time **24 hours** | 🍲 Prep time **15 minutes** | ⏰ Function time **1,5 minutes** | 🕐 Servings **4** | 🔥 Calories **310** | Complexity **Intermediate** |

Tags: Creamy, Sweet, Adults Only   **Ninja CREAMi function:** Ice Cream

Tools needed: Large bowl, whisk, measuring cups and spoons, Ninja CREAMi pint

Ingredients:

- 1 tablespoon cream cheese
- 1 cup heavy cream
- 1 cup whole milk
- 1/2 cup granulated sugar
- 1/4 cup strong brewed espresso, cooled
- 1 teaspoon vanilla extract

Directions:

1. Soften the cream cheese in the microwave for 10 seconds.
2. In a large bowl, combine the softened cream cheese, heavy cream, whole milk, granulated sugar, cooled espresso, vanilla extract, and a pinch of salt. Whisk until smooth.
3. Transfer the mixture to the Ninja CREAMi pint container.
4. Freeze the pint for 24 hours to ensure a solid freeze.
5. Before using, remove the CREAMi Pint lid.
6. Place the frozen pint in the Ninja CREAMi.
7. Select the 'Ice Cream' function and process for 1.5 minutes.
8. After processing, check the ice cream consistency. For a firmer texture, opt for the 'Re-spin' cycle.
9. Serve immediately or store in an airtight container in the freezer.

Nutritional Information (per serving): Protein: 3g | Carbohydrates: 26g | Sodium: 85mg | Potassium: 120mg | Sugar: 24g

Raspberry & Mint Ice Cream

Flavor profile: Bright and refreshing with the tartness of raspberries and a fresh, cool hint of mint.
Best for occasions: +

❄️ Freeze time	🍲 Prep time	⏰ Function time	⏱️ Servings	🔥 Calories	Complexity
24 hours	**15 minutes**	**1,5 minutes**	**4**	**280**	**Intermediate**

Tags: Refreshing, Creamy, Fruity, Herbal   **Ninja CREAMi function:** Ice Cream

Tools needed: Large bowl, whisk, measuring cups and spoons, Ninja CREAMi pint

Ingredients:

- 1 tablespoon cream cheese
- 1 cup heavy cream
- 1 cup whole milk
- 1/2 cup granulated sugar
- 1 cup fresh raspberries
- 1/4 cup fresh mint leaves, finely chopped

Directions:

1. Soften the cream cheese in the microwave for 10 seconds.
2. In a large bowl, whisk together the softened cream cheese, heavy cream, whole milk, granulated sugar, raspberries, chopped mint, and a pinch of salt until well combined.
3. Pour the mixture into the Ninja CREAMi pint container.
4. Freeze the pint for 24 hours to ensure a thorough freeze.
5. Before using, remove the CREAMi Pint lid.
6. Insert the frozen pint into the Ninja CREAMi.
7. Select the 'Ice Cream' function and process for 1.5 minutes.
8. Check the consistency after processing. If a firmer texture is desired, run the 'Re-spin' cycle.
9. Serve immediately or store in an airtight container in the freezer.

Nutritional Information (per serving): Protein: 3g | Carbohydrates: 22g | Sodium: 75mg | Potassium: 125mg | Sugar: 20g

Caramelized Banana Ice Cream

Flavor profile: Rich and sweet with the deep, caramel-like taste of cooked bananas, complemented by a creamy backdrop.
Best for occasions: Winter Comfort

❄️ Freeze time **24 hours**	🍲 Prep time **25 minutes**	⏰ Function time **1,5 minutes**	🥧 Servings **4**	🔥 Calories **320**	Complexity **Intermediate**

Tags: Sweet, Creamy

Ninja CREAMi function: Ice Cream

Tools needed: Large bowl, whisk, frying pan, measuring cups and spoons, Ninja CREAMi pint

Ingredients:

- 1 tablespoon cream cheese
- 2 ripe bananas, sliced and caramelized
- 1 cup heavy cream
- 1 cup whole milk
- 1/2 cup brown sugar
- 1 teaspoon vanilla extract

Directions:

1. Soften the cream cheese in the microwave for 10 seconds.
2. Caramelize the banana slices in a frying pan with a bit of brown sugar until golden and soft.
3. In a large bowl, combine the softened cream cheese, caramelized bananas, heavy cream, whole milk, brown sugar, vanilla extract, and a pinch of salt. Whisk until well combined.
4. Pour the mixture into the Ninja CREAMi pint container.
5. Freeze the pint for 24 hours to ensure a thorough freeze.
6. Before using, remove the CREAMi Pint lid.
7. Insert the frozen pint into the Ninja CREAMi.
8. Select the 'Ice Cream' function and process for 1.5 minutes.
9. Check the consistency after processing. For a firmer texture, run the 'Re-spin' cycle.
10. Serve immediately or store in an airtight container in the freezer.

Nutritional Information (per serving): Protein: 4g | Carbohydrates: 34g | Sodium: 85mg | Potassium: 300mg | Sugar: 30g

---

Red Velvet Ice Cream

Flavor profile: Rich cocoa with a tangy twist, enveloped in creamy sweetness and the iconic red velvet color.
Best for occasions: Birthday Parties

❄️ Freeze time **24 hours**	🍲 Prep time **20 minutes**	⏰ Function time **1,5 minutes**	🥧 Servings **4**	🔥 Calories **310**	Complexity **Beginner**

Tags: Sweet, Creamy, Kid Friendly

Ninja CREAMi function: Ice Cream

Tools needed: Large bowl, whisk, measuring cups and spoons, Ninja CREAMi pint

Ingredients:

- 1 tablespoon cream cheese, softened
- 1 cup heavy cream
- 1 cup whole milk
- 1/2 cup granulated sugar
- 2 tablespoons unsweetened cocoa powder
- 1 teaspoon red food coloring
- 1 teaspoon vanilla extract

Directions:

1. Soften the cream cheese in the microwave for 10 seconds.
2. In a large bowl, whisk together the softened cream cheese, heavy cream, whole milk, sugar, cocoa powder, red food coloring, vanilla extract, and a pinch of salt until smooth and well combined.
3. Pour the mixture into the Ninja CREAMi pint container.
4. Freeze the pint for 24 hours to ensure a solid freeze.
5. Before using, remove the CREAMi Pint lid.
6. Insert the frozen pint into the Ninja CREAMi.
7. Select the 'Ice Cream' function and process for 1.5 minutes.
8. Check the consistency after processing. For a firmer texture, run the 'Re-spin' cycle.
9. Serve immediately or store in an airtight container in the freezer.

Nutritional Information (per serving): Protein: 3g | Carbohydrates: 28g | Sodium: 85mg | Potassium: 150mg | Sugar: 25g

Matcha Green Tea Ice Cream

Flavor profile: Rich and creamy with the distinctive earthy notes of matcha, balanced by the smooth, custard-like texture of the egg yolks.
Best for occasions: Health-Conscious Gatherings

| ❄️ Freeze time **24 hours** | 🍲 Prep time **20 minutes** | ⏰ Function time **1,5 minutes** | 🕐 Servings **4** | 🔥 Calories **350** | Complexity **Advanced** |

Tags: Creamy, Sweet, Vegetarian   ***Ninja CREAMi function:*** Ice Cream

Tools needed: Large bowl, whisk, saucepan, measuring cups and spoons, Ninja CREAMi pint

Ingredients:

- 1 tablespoon cream cheese, softened
- 1 cup heavy cream
- 1 cup whole milk
- 1/2 cup granulated sugar
- 2 tablespoons matcha green tea powder
- 4 egg yolks

Directions:

1. Soften the cream cheese in the microwave for 10 seconds.
2. In a saucepan, combine heavy cream, whole milk, and matcha green tea powder. Heat over medium heat until the mixture is warm but not boiling.
3. In a separate bowl, whisk together egg yolks and sugar until light and fluffy. Gradually pour the warm matcha cream mixture into the egg yolks, whisking continuously to temper the eggs.
4. Return the mixture to the saucepan and heat over low heat, stirring constantly until the mixture thickens and coats the back of a spoon.
5. Remove from heat and stir in the softened cream cheese. Mix until smooth. Strain the mixture through a fine-mesh sieve into a bowl to remove lumps.
6. Cool the mixture to room temperature, then pour it into the Ninja CREAMi pint container. Freeze the pint for 24 hours to ensure a thorough freeze. Before using, remove the CREAMi Pint lid.
7. Insert the frozen pint into the Ninja CREAMi.
8. Select the 'Ice Cream' function and process for 1.5 minutes.
9. Check the consistency after processing. For a firmer texture, run the 'Respin' cycle. Serve immediately or store in an airtight container in the freezer.

Nutritional Information (per serving): Protein: 6g | Carbohydrates: 28g | Sodium: 85mg | Potassium: 170mg | Sugar: 25g

Spiced Chai Ice Cream

Flavor profile: A harmonious blend of black tea and exotic spices like cardamom, cinnamon, and ginger, all mellowed by the richness of cream.
Best for occasions: Winter Comfort

❄ Freeze time **24 hours**	🍲 Prep time **30 minutes**	🕐 Function time **1,5 minutes**	🍕 Servings **4**	🔥 Calories **250**	Complexity **Intermediate**

Tags: Spiced, Creamy, Sweet   ***Ninja CREAMi function:*** Ice Cream

Tools needed: Saucepan, Fine-mesh strainer, Whisk, Large bowl, Measuring cups and spoons, Ninja CREAMi

Ingredients:

- 1 cup heavy cream
- 1/2 cup whole milk
- 3/8 cup granulated sugar
- 1 tablespoon loose black tea leaves or 2 black tea bags
- 1/2 teaspoon ground cardamom
- 1/4 teaspoon ground cinnamon
- 1/8 teaspoon ground ginger
- 1/8 teaspoon ground cloves
- 1/8 teaspoon ground nutmeg
- Pinch of salt
- 1 tablespoon cream cheese, softened

Directions:

1. In a saucepan, simmer the milk and add the tea leaves or bags, cardamom, cinnamon, ginger, cloves, and nutmeg.
2. After simmering for 5 minutes, remove from heat and steep for 10 minutes.
3. Strain the mixture into a large bowl and dissolve the sugar into it.
4. Mix in the heavy cream and a pinch of salt.
5. Soften the cream cheese in the microwave for 10 seconds and then whisk into the milk mixture until smooth.
6. Pour into the CREAMi Pint, secure the lid, and freeze for 24 hours.
7. Before churning, remove the CREAMi Pint lid and insert it into the Ninja CREAMi.
8. Process using the 'Ice Cream' function for 1.5 minutes.
9. Serve immediately for a soft consistency or freeze for 1-2 hours for a firmer texture.

Nutritional Information (per serving): Protein: 2g | Carbohydrates: 20g | Sodium: 60mg | Potassium: 50mg | Sugar: 19g

---

Bourbon Vanilla Bean Ice Cream

Flavor profile: A sophisticated blend of warm bourbon and aromatic vanilla with a smooth and creamy texture.
Best for occasions: Fancy Dinner Parties, Adults Only

❄ Freeze time **24 hours**	🍲 Prep time **20 minutes**	🕐 Function time **1,5 minutes**	🍕 Servings **4**	🔥 Calories **260**	Complexity **Beginner**

Tags: Tags: Creamy, Sweet, Adults Only, Rich Flavor   ***Ninja CREAMi function:*** Ice Cream

Tools needed: Large bowl, Whisk, Measuring cups and spoons, Ninja CREAMi

Ingredients:

- 1 cup heavy cream
- 1/2 cup whole milk
- 3/8 cup granulated sugar
- 1 teaspoon bourbon
- 1 vanilla bean, split lengthwise and seeds scraped
- 1 ounce cream cheese, softened

Directions:

1. In a large bowl, combine the heavy cream, whole milk, and granulated sugar.
2. Add the scraped seeds from the vanilla bean to the mixture, along with the bourbon and a pinch of salt.
3. Microwave the cream cheese for 10 seconds, then whisk it until no lumps remain.
4. Pour the mixture into the CREAMi Pint, secure the lid, and freeze for 24 hours.
5. Remove the CREAMi Pint lid before inserting it into the Ninja CREAMi.
6. Choose the Ice Cream function on the Ninja CREAMi and churn for 1.5 minutes.
7. Serve immediately for a soft texture or place in the freezer for 1-2 hours for a scoopable consistency.

Nutritional Information (per serving): Protein: 2g | Carbohydrates: 20g | Sodium: 60mg | Potassium: 50mg | Sugar: 28g

Honey Lavender Ice Cream

Flavor profile: Sweet and floral with the delicate essence of lavender and honey's rich, natural sweetness.
Best for occasions: Fancy Dinner Parties

❄ Freeze time **24 hours**	🍲 Prep time **20 minutes**	⏰ Function time **1,5 minutes**	⏱ Servings **4**	🔥 Calories **370**	—o Complexity **Intermediate**

Tags: Floral, Sweet, Creamy

Ninja CREAMi function: Ice Cream

Tools needed: Large bowl, saucepan, whisk, measuring cups and spoons, Ninja CREAMi pint

Ingredients:

- 1 tablespoon cream cheese, softened
- 1 cup heavy cream
- 1 cup whole milk
- 1/2 cup honey
- 1 tablespoon dried lavender flowers
- 4 egg yolks

Directions:

1. Soften the cream cheese in the microwave for 10 seconds.
2. In a saucepan, combine heavy cream, whole milk, honey, and dried lavender flowers. Heat over medium heat until warm but not boiling. Allow the lavender to infuse for about 5 minutes, then strain to remove the flowers.
3. In a separate bowl, whisk together egg yolks until light and fluffy.
4. Gradually pour the warm lavender-infused cream mixture into the egg yolks, whisking continuously to temper the eggs.
5. Return the mixture to the saucepan and heat over low heat, stirring constantly, until it thickens and coats the back of a spoon.
6. Remove from heat and stir in the softened cream cheese and a pinch of salt. Mix until smooth. Strain the mixture through a fine-mesh sieve into a bowl to remove lumps. Cool the mixture to room temperature, then pour it into the Ninja CREAMi pint container. Freeze the pint for 24 hours to ensure a thorough freeze.
7. Before using, remove the CREAMi Pint lid. Insert the frozen pint into the Ninja CREAMi. Select the 'Ice Cream' function and process for 1.5 minutes.
8. Check the consistency after processing. For a firmer texture, run the 'Re-spin' cycle. Serve immediately or store in an airtight container in the freezer.

Nutritional Information (per serving): Protein: 5g | Carbohydrates: 28g | Sodium: 70mg | Potassium: 180mg | Sugar: 26g

Coconut & Turmeric Ice Cream

Flavor profile: Creamy and rich with a hint of warm, earthy turmeric, complemented by the tropical taste of coconut.
Best for occasions: Health-Conscious Gatherings

❄️ Freeze time	Prep time	Function time	Servings	Calories	Complexity
24 hours	**20 minutes**	**1,5 minutes**	**4**	**360**	**Advanced**

Tags: Dairy Free, Vegan, Lite, Refreshing

Ninja CREAMi function: Ice Cream

Tools needed: Large bowl, saucepan, whisk, measuring cups and spoons, Ninja CREAMi pint

Ingredients:

- 1 tablespoon cream cheese, softened
- 1 cup canned coconut milk
- 1 cup heavy cream
- 1/2 cup granulated sugar
- 1 teaspoon turmeric powder
- 4 egg yolks
- Pinch of black pepper (to enhance turmeric absorption)
- Pinch of salt

Directions:

1. Soften the cream cheese in the microwave for 10 seconds.
2. In a saucepan, combine coconut milk, heavy cream, turmeric powder, and a pinch of black pepper. Heat over medium heat until warm but not boiling. In a separate bowl, whisk together egg yolks and sugar until light and fluffy.
3. Gradually pour the warm coconut-turmeric mixture into the egg yolks, whisking continuously to temper the eggs. Return the mixture to the saucepan and heat over low heat, stirring constantly, until the mixture thickens and coats the back of a spoon.
4. Remove from heat and stir in the softened cream cheese and a pinch of salt. Mix until smooth. Strain the mixture through a fine-mesh sieve into a bowl to remove lumps.
5. Cool the mixture to room temperature, then pour it into the Ninja CREAMi pint container. Freeze the pint for 24 hours to ensure a thorough freeze.
6. Before using, remove the CREAMi Pint lid. Insert the frozen pint into the Ninja CREAMi. Select the 'Ice Cream' function and process for 1.5 minutes.
7. Check the consistency after processing. For a firmer texture, run the 'Re-spin' cycle. Serve immediately or store in an airtight container in the freezer.

Nutritional Information (per serving): Protein: 5g | Carbohydrates: 20g | Sodium: 60mg | Potassium: 200mg | Sugar: 18g

Salted Caramel & Pecan Ice Cream

Flavor profile: Creamy caramel with a hint of salt and crunchy pecan pieces.
Best for occasions: Fancy Dinner Parties, Adults Only

❄️ Freeze time	Prep time	Function time	Servings	Calories	Complexity
24 hours	**20 minutes**	**2 minutes**	**4**	**480**	**Intermediate**

Tags: Creamy, Sweet, Nutty

Ninja CREAMi function: Ice Cream

Tools needed: Saucepan, baking sheet, blender or food processor, mixing bowl, measuring cups, measuring spoons

Ingredients:

- 1 cup heavy cream
- 1 cup whole milk
- 3/4 cup granulated sugar
- 1/2 cup caramel sauce (plus extra for drizzling)
- 1/2 teaspoon sea salt
- 1 cup pecans, toasted and chopped

Directions:

1. In a saucepan over medium heat, combine heavy cream, whole milk, and sugar. Stir continuously until the sugar dissolves and the mixture is just about to simmer. Remove from heat and let cool. Stir in caramel sauce and sea salt into the cooled cream mixture. Adjust salt to taste for that perfect salty-sweet balance.
2. Pour the mixture into a CREAMi Pint and secure with the Outer Bowl and Lid. Place the pint in the freezer and freeze until solid, typically for 24 hours.
3. Preheat your oven to 350°F (175°C). Spread pecans on a baking sheet and toast in the oven for about 10 minutes, or until they are aromatic and slightly browned. Allow to cool, then chop roughly.
4. Once the ice cream base is frozen, attach the Creamerizer Paddle to the Motor Base, and place the frozen pint into the Outer Bowl. Secure the Lid.
5. Select the "Ice Cream" function on the Control Panel and start the process. Halfway through churning, add the toasted chopped pecans.
6. Continue to churn until the mixture reaches a smooth, creamy consistency.
7. Serve immediately for a soft-serve texture, or transfer to an airtight container and freeze for an additional 1-2 hours for a firmer texture. Drizzle with extra caramel sauce and sprinkle a few sea salt flakes before serving if desired.

Nutritional Information (per serving): Protein: 5g | Carbohydrates: 40g | Sodium: 300mg | Potassium: 130mg | Sugar: 35g

Pecan Pie Ice Cream

Flavor profile: Buttery and nutty with a sweet, caramel-like richness complemented by the crunch of toasted pecans.
Best for occasions: Holiday Celebrations

❄ Freeze time **24 hours**	⏱ Prep time **20 minutes**	⏰ Function time **Ice Cream - 1.5 minutes, Mix-in - 1 minute**

Servings **4**	Calories **360**	Complexity **Intermediate**

Tags: Nutty, Sweet, Creamy

Ninja CREAMi function: Ice Cream, Mix-in

Tools needed: Large bowl, Whisk, Measuring cups, Measuring spoons, Ninja CREAMi

Ingredients:

- 1 cup heavy cream
- 1/2 cup whole milk
- 6 tablespoons brown sugar
- 4 tablespoons dark corn syrup
- 3 tablespoons chopped pecans, toasted, plus extra for mix-in
- 3 tablespoons pie crust pieces
- 1 tablespoon cream cheese, softened
- 1 teaspoon vanilla extract
- 1 tablespoon maple syrup

Directions:

1. In a large bowl, combine heavy cream, whole milk, brown sugar, dark corn syrup, vanilla extract, and maple syrup. Whisk until the sugar is dissolved.
2. Soften the cream cheese in the microwave for 10 seconds, then whisk into the cream mixture until smooth.
3. Stir in the toasted chopped pecans.
4. Pour the mixture into the CREAMi Pint and freeze for 24 hours.
5. Remove the CREAMi Pint lid and insert it into the Ninja CREAMi. Churn using the 'Ice Cream' function for 1.5 minutes.
6. After churning, with a spoon, create a 1½-inch wide hole that reaches the bottom of the pint.
7. Add additional toasted pecans and pie crust pieces into the hole.
8. Use the 'Mix-in' function for an additional 1 minute.
9. Serve immediately for a soft-serve texture, or transfer to the freezer for 1-2 hours for a firmer consistency.

Nutritional Information (per serving): Protein: 3g | Carbohydrates: 30g | Sodium: 90mg | Potassium: 115mg | Sugar: 28g

Mojito Sorbet

Flavor profile: Bright and zesty lime, aromatic fresh mint, with the subtle warmth of rum, all in a light and refreshing sorbet.
Best for occasions: Summer Gatherings

| ❄️ Freeze time **24 hours** | 🍲 Prep time **15 minutes** | ⏰ Function time **Ice Cream - 1.5 minutes, Mix-in - 1 minute** | 📐 Servings **4** | 🔥 Calories **220** | —○ Complexity **Beginner** |

Tags: Vegan, Refreshing, Lite

Ninja CREAMi function: Ice Cream, Mix-in

Tools needed: Large bowl, Whisk, Measuring cups, Measuring spoons, Ninja CREAMi

Ingredients:

- 1 1/2 cups water
- 1 cup granulated sugar
- 1/2 cup fresh lime juice
- 1 tablespoon lime zest
- 1 tablespoon fresh mint leaves, finely chopped
- 1 tablespoon white rum
- 1 tablespoon cream cheese, softened
- Additional mint leaves for mix-in
- Extra lime zest for mix-in

Directions:

1. In a saucepan over medium heat, combine water and sugar, stirring until the sugar dissolves to create a simple syrup. Let cool.
2. Stir in the lime juice, zest, chopped mint leaves, and white rum into the cooled syrup.
3. Soften the cream cheese in the microwave for 10 seconds and whisk into the lime and mint mixture until smooth.
4. Pour the mixture into the CREAMi Pint and freeze for 24 hours.
5. Remove the CREAMi Pint lid and place the pint into the Ninja CREAMi—process using the 'Ice Cream' function for 1.5 minutes.
6. After processing, with a spoon, create a 1½-inch wide hole that reaches the bottom of the pint.
7. Add additional mint leaves and lime zest into the hole.
8. Use the 'Mix-in' function for an additional 1 minute.
9. Serve immediately to enjoy a refreshingly cool sorbet.

Nutritional Information (per serving): Protein: 0g | Carbohydrates: 50g | Sodium: 15mg | Potassium: 20mg | Sugar: 49g

---

Black Forest Gateau Ice Cream

Flavor profile: Rich chocolate, tart cherries, and the subtle sweetness of cake combined with the creamy texture of classic ice cream.
Best for occasions: Romantic Occasions

| ❄️ Freeze time **24 hours** | 🍲 Prep time **25 minutes** | ⏰ Function time **Ice Cream - 1.5 minutes, Mix-in - 1 minute** | 📐 Servings **4** | 🔥 Calories **350** | —● Complexity **Advanced** |

Tags: Fruity, Sweet, Creamy

Ninja CREAMi function: Ice Cream, Mix-in

Tools needed: Large bowl, Whisk, Measuring cups, Measuring spoons, Ninja CREAMi

Ingredients:

- 1 cup heavy cream
- 1/2 cup whole milk
- 6 tablespoons granulated sugar
- 4 tablespoons cocoa powder
- 3 tablespoons cherry preserves
- 3 tablespoons chocolate cake, crumbled
- 2 tablespoons dark chocolate shavings
- 1 tablespoon cream cheese, softened
- 1 teaspoon vanilla extract

Directions:

1. Whisk together the heavy cream, whole milk, granulated sugar, cocoa powder, and vanilla extract in a large bowl until fully combined.
2. Soften the cream cheese in the microwave for 10 seconds and then mix into the cream base until smooth.
3. Pour the mixture into the CREAMi Pint and freeze for 24 hours.
4. Remove the CREAMi Pint lid and place the pint into the Ninja CREAM. Process using the 'Ice Cream' function for 1.5 minutes.
5. After churning, with a spoon, create a 1½-inch wide hole that reaches the bottom of the pint.
6. Spoon cherry preserves into the hole, then sprinkle in the crumbled chocolate cake and dark chocolate shavings.
7. Replace the lid and use the 'Mix-in' function for an additional 1 minute.
8. Serve immediately for a soft serve texture or place in the freezer for 1-2 hours for a more traditional ice cream consistency.

Nutritional Information (per serving): Protein: 3g | Carbohydrates: 32g | Sodium: 80mg | Potassium: 120mg | Sugar: 30g

Blueberry Pancake Ice Cream

Flavor profile: Sweet and comforting notes of maple and vanilla, paired with the bright burst of blueberry and the satisfying texture of pancake pieces.
Best for occasions: Breakfast, Kids' Fun Day

| ❄ Freeze time **24 hours** | 🍲 Prep time **20 minutes** | ⏰ Function time **Ice Cream - 1.5 minutes, Mix-in - 1 minute** | 🕐 Servings **4** | 🔥 Calories **320** | Complexity **Beginner** |

Tags: Sweet, Fruity, Creamy   **Ninja CREAMi function:** Ice Cream, Mix-in

Tools needed: Large bowl, Whisk, Measuring cups, Measuring spoons, Ninja CREAMi

Ingredients:

- 1 cup heavy cream
- 1/2 cup whole milk
- 6 tablespoons maple syrup
- 4 tablespoons blueberry jam
- 3 tablespoons pancake pieces, toasted and cooled
- 1 tablespoon cream cheese, softened
- 1 teaspoon vanilla extract
- Additional pancake pieces for mix-in
- Extra blueberry jam for mix-in

Directions:

1. In a large bowl, mix the heavy cream, whole milk, maple syrup, and vanilla extract until well combined.
2. Soften the cream cheese in the microwave for 10 seconds and whisk it into the milk mixture until smooth.
3. Gently fold in the 3 tablespoons of blueberry jam, creating a marbled effect.
4. Pour the mixture into the CREAMi Pint and freeze for 24 hours.
5. After freezing, remove the lid from the CREAMi Pint and insert the pint into the Ninja CREAMi. Churn using the 'Ice Cream' function for 1.5 minutes.
6. Once churned, with a spoon, create a 1½-inch wide hole that reaches the bottom of the pint. Insert additional pancake pieces and dollops of blueberry jam into the hole.
7. Use the 'Mix-in' function for an additional 1 minute to distribute the mix-ins.
8. Serve immediately for a soft-serve texture, or place in the freezer for 1-2 hours for a firmer consistency.

Nutritional Information (per serving): Protein: 3g | Carbohydrates: 34g | Sodium: 70mg | Potassium: 100mg | Sugar: 31g

White Chocolate Raspberry Ice Cream

Flavor profile: Creamy and sweet white chocolate balanced by the tangy and fruity sharpness of raspberries, enhanced by the delightful textures of the mix-ins.
Best for occasions: Kids' Fun Day

❄️ Freeze time **24 hours**	Prep time **20 minutes**	Function time **Ice Cream - 1.5 minutes, Mix-in - 1 minute**	Servings **4**	Calories **360**	Complexity **Intermediate**

Tags: Sweet, Fruity, Creamy

Ninja CREAMi function: Ice Cream, Mix-in

Tools needed: Large bowl, Whisk, Measuring cups, Measuring spoons, Ninja CREAMi

Ingredients:

- 1 cup heavy cream
- 1/2 cup whole milk
- 6 tablespoons granulated sugar
- 4 tablespoons white chocolate chips, melted
- 3 tablespoons raspberry preserves
- 3 tablespoons white chocolate chips for mix-in
- 1 tablespoon cream cheese, softened
- 1 teaspoon vanilla extract

Directions:

1. Combine the heavy cream, whole milk, and sugar in a large bowl, whisking until the sugar dissolves.
2. Stir in the melted white chocolate and vanilla extract until the mixture is uniform.
3. Microwave the cream cheese for 10 seconds, then whisk into the mixture until smooth.
4. Pour the base into the CREAMi Pint and freeze for 24 hours.
5. Remove the lid from the CREAMi Pint and insert the pint into the Ninja CREAMi. Churn using the 'Ice Cream' function for 1.5 minutes.
6. With a spoon, create a 1½-inch wide hole reaching the pint's bottom.
7. Spoon raspberry preserves into the hole and add white chocolate chips. Use the 'Mix-in' function for an additional 1 minute.
8. Serve immediately for a soft-serve texture or freeze for 1-2 hours for a firmer consistency.

Nutritional Information (per serving): Protein: 3g | Carbohydrates: 35g | Sodium: 85mg | Potassium: 110mg | Sugar: 32g

---

Almond Joy Ice Cream

Flavor profile: A tropical sweetness from coconut, the richness of milk chocolate, and the nutty crunch of almonds, all combined in a smooth ice cream.
Best for occasions: Movie Night, Kids' Fun Day

❄️ Freeze time **24 hours**	Prep time **20 minutes**	Function time **Ice Cream - 1.5 minutes, Mix-in - 1 minute**	Servings **4**	Calories **350**	Complexity **Intermediate**

Tags: Nutty, Sweet, Creamy, Dairy Free

Ninja CREAMi function: Ice Cream, Mix-in

Tools needed: Large bowl, Whisk, Measuring cups, Measuring spoons, Ninja CREAMi

Ingredients:

- 1 cup heavy cream
- 1/2 cup coconut milk
- 6 tablespoons granulated sugar
- 4 tablespoons shredded sweetened coconut
- 3 tablespoons milk chocolate chips, melted
- 3 tablespoons whole almonds, chopped, plus extra for mix-in
- 1 tablespoon cream cheese, softened
- 1 teaspoon coconut extract

Directions:

1. In a large bowl, combine the heavy cream, coconut milk, granulated sugar, and coconut extract, whisking until the sugar is fully dissolved.
2. Warm the cream cheese in the microwave for 10 seconds, then blend into the mixture until smooth.
3. Stir in the melted milk chocolate until the mixture is homogenous.
4. Add the shredded coconut and chopped almonds, stirring to distribute evenly. Pour the base into the CREAMi Pint and freeze for 24 hours.
5. After freezing, remove the CREAMi Pint lid and place the pint into the Ninja CREAMi. Churn using the 'Ice Cream' function for 1.5 minutes.
6. With a spoon, create a 1½-inch wide hole reaching the pint's bottom.
7. Add extra chopped almonds into the hole. Process with the 'Mix-in' function for an additional 1 minute to incorporate the mix-ins.
8. Serve immediately for a soft texture or place in the freezer for 1-2 hours for a firmer consistency.

Nutritional Information (per serving): Protein: 4g | Carbohydrates: 25g | Sodium: 70mg | Potassium: 150mg | Sugar: 22g

Chocolate Hazelnut Spread Ice Cream

Flavor profile: Rich and chocolatey with a full-bodied hazelnut undertone, complemented by the texture of chopped hazelnuts and chocolate pieces.
Best for occasions: Kids' Fun Day, Winter Comfort

❄ Freeze time **24 hours**	Prep time **20 minutes**	Function time **Ice Cream - 1.5 minutes, Mix-in - 1 minute**	Servings **4**	Calories **380**	Complexity **Beginner**

Tags: Sweet, Nutty, Creamy   **Ninja CREAMi function:** Ice Cream, Mix-in

Tools needed: Large bowl, Whisk, Measuring cups, Measuring spoons, Ninja CREAMi

Ingredients:

- 1 cup heavy cream
- 1/2 cup whole milk
- 6 tablespoons chocolate hazelnut spread
- 4 tablespoons chopped hazelnuts, plus extra for mix-in
- 3 tablespoons chocolate chips for mix-in
- 1 tablespoon cream cheese, softened
- 1 teaspoon vanilla extract

Directions:

1. Whisk together the heavy cream, whole milk, chocolate hazelnut spread, and vanilla extract in a large bowl until well combined.
2. Microwave the cream cheese for 10 seconds and then whisk it until no lumps remain.
3. Pour the base into the CREAMi Pint and freeze for 24 hours.
4. After freezing, remove the lid from the CREAMi Pint and insert the pint into the Ninja CREAMi. Churn using the 'Ice Cream' function for 1.5 minutes.
5. With a spoon, create a 1½-inch wide hole reaching the pint's bottom.
6. Add extra chopped hazelnuts and chocolate chips into the hole.
7. Use the 'Mix-in' function for an additional 1 minute to incorporate the mix-ins.
8. Serve immediately for a soft-serve texture or transfer to the freezer for 1-2 hours for a firmer consistency.

Nutritional Information (per serving): Protein: 5g | Carbohydrates: 28g | Sodium: 90mg | Potassium: 200mg | Sugar: 27g

Birthday Cake Ice Cream

Flavor profile: Sweet vanilla and buttery notes of cake batter, interspersed with the fun crunch of rainbow sprinkles and soft, rich cake pieces.
Best for occasions: Birthday Parties

| ❄️ Freeze time **24 hours** | 🍲 Prep time **20 minutes** | ⏰ Function time **Ice Cream - 1.5 minutes, Mix-in - 1 minute** | 🥧 Servings **4** | 🔥 Calories **360** | Complexity **Beginner** |

Tags: Sweet, Kid Friendly

Ninja CREAMi function: Ice Cream, Mix-in

Tools needed: Large bowl, Whisk, Measuring cups, Measuring spoons, Ninja CREAMi

Ingredients:

- 1 cup heavy cream
- 1/2 cup whole milk
- 6 tablespoons granulated sugar
- 4 tablespoons cake mix (vanilla or butter flavor)
- 3 tablespoons rainbow sprinkles, plus extra for mix-in
- 3 tablespoons vanilla cake, cubed, plus extra for mix-in
- 1 tablespoon cream cheese, softened
- 1 teaspoon vanilla extract

Directions:

1. In a large bowl, combine the heavy cream, whole milk, sugar, cake mix, and vanilla extract. Whisk until the sugar and cake mix are entirely dissolved. Microwave the cream cheese for 10 seconds, then blend into the mixture until smooth.
2. Stir in the 3 tablespoons of rainbow sprinkles and cubed vanilla cake pieces. Pour the mixture into the CREAMi Pint and place it in the freezer for 24 hours.
3. Remove the lid from the frozen CREAMi Pint and insert it into the Ninja CREAMi. Churn using the 'Ice Cream' function for 1.5 minutes.
4. After churning, use a spoon to create a 1½-inch wide hole that reaches the bottom of the pint.
5. Layer extra rainbow sprinkles and cake cubes into the hole.
6. Close the lid and use the 'Mix-in' function for an additional 1 minute to blend the mix-ins throughout the ice cream.
7. Serve immediately for a soft texture or freeze for 1-2 hours for a scoopable consistency.

Nutritional Information (per serving): Protein: 3g | Carbohydrates: 38g | Sodium: 150mg | Potassium: 120mg | Sugar: 36g

---

Espresso Bean & Toffee Ice Cream

Flavor profile: Deep and rich with coffee notes, sweet buttery toffee, and a luxurious creamy backdrop punctuated by the satisfying crunch of toffee bits.
Best for occasions: Adults Only, Fancy Dinner Parties

| ❄️ Freeze time **24 hours** | 🍲 Prep time **20 minutes** | ⏰ Function time **Ice Cream - 1.5 minutes, Mix-in - 1 minute** | 🥧 Servings **4** | 🔥 Calories **320** | Complexity **Intermediate** |

Tags: Sweet, Creamy, Adults Only

Ninja CREAMi function: Ice Cream, Mix-in

Tools needed: Large bowl, Whisk, Measuring cups, Measuring spoons, Ninja CREAMi

Ingredients:

- 1 cup heavy cream
- 1/2 cup whole milk
- 6 tablespoons granulated sugar
- 3 tablespoons strong brewed espresso, cooled
- 3 tablespoons toffee bits, plus extra for mix-in
- 1 tablespoon cream cheese, softened
- 1 teaspoon vanilla extract

Directions:

1. In a large bowl, combine the granulated sugar, cooled espresso, vanilla extract, and salt. Stir until the sugar has dissolved. Pour in the heavy cream and whole milk, whisking until fully combined.
2. Microwave the cream cheese for 10 seconds, then whisk into the cream mixture until smooth.
3. Transfer the mixture to the CREAMi Pint and freeze for 24 hours.
4. Remove the CREAMi Pint lid and insert the pint into the Ninja CREAMi.
5. Select the 'Ice Cream' function and process for 1.5 minutes.
6. Create a 1½ -inch wide hole reaching the pint's bottom with a spoon.
7. Add toffee bits as mix-ins and use the Mix-in function for an extra 1 minute.
8. Serve immediately for a soft serve texture or a more traditional ice cream consistency; place in the freezer for 1-2 hours.

Nutritional Information (per serving): Protein: 2g | Carbohydrates: 28g | Sodium: 80mg | Potassium: 105mg | Sugar: 26g

S'mores Ice Cream

Flavor profile: The quintessential taste of s'mores - gooey marshmallows, rich chocolate, and the honeyed crunch of graham crackers, all swirled into a velvety ice cream base.
Best for occasions: Kids' Fun Day, Movie Night

❄ Freeze time **24 hours**	Prep time **20 minutes**	Function time **Ice Cream - 1.5 minutes, Mix-in - 1 minute**	Servings **4**	Calories **350**

Complexity **Beginner**

Tags: Sweet, Creamy, Kid Friendly   ***Ninja CREAMi function:*** Ice Cream, Mix-in

Tools needed: Large bowl, Whisk, Measuring cups, Measuring spoons, Ninja CREAMi

Ingredients:

- 1 cup heavy cream
- 1/2 cup whole milk
- 6 tablespoons granulated sugar
- 4 tablespoons cocoa powder
- 3 tablespoons marshmallow fluff
- 3 tablespoons crushed graham crackers, plus extra for mix-in
- 2 tablespoons chocolate chips, plus different for mix-in
- 1 tablespoon cream cheese, softened
- 1 teaspoon vanilla extract

Directions:

1. In a large bowl, whisk together the heavy cream, whole milk, granulated sugar, cocoa powder, and vanilla extract until well combined.
2. Microwave the cream cheese for 10 seconds and then whisk into the mixture until there are no lumps.
3. Stir in the marshmallow fluff until it's evenly distributed.
4. Pour the mixture into the CREAMi Pint and freeze for 24 hours.
5. Remove the CREAMi Pint lid and place the pint into the Ninja CREAMi.
6. Use the 'Ice Cream' function and churn for 1.5 minutes.
7. After churning, with a spoon, create a 1½-inch wide hole that reaches the bottom of the pint.
8. Add extra crushed graham crackers and chocolate chips into the hole as mix-ins.
9. Use the 'Mix-in' function for an additional 1 minute.
10. Serve immediately for a soft texture or freeze for an additional 1-2 hours for a more traditional ice cream consistency.

Nutritional Information (per serving): Protein: 3g | Carbohydrates: 34g | Sodium: 90mg | Potassium: 110mg | Sugar: 29g

Berry Bliss Lite Ice Cream

Flavor profile: A delightful blend of sweet and tangy flavors from a mix of fresh berries, complemented by Greek yogurt's creamy, slightly sour taste.
Best for occasions: Health-Conscious Gatherings

❄ Freeze time **24 hours**	⏲ Prep time **15 minutes**	⏰ Function time **1.5 minutes**	Servings **4**	Calories **180**	Complexity **Beginner**

Tags: Lite, Fruity, Vegetarian　　　　　　**Ninja CREAMi function:** Lite Ice Cream
Tools needed: Large bowl, Blender, Measuring cups, Measuring spoons, Ninja CREAMi

Ingredients:

- 2 cups skim milk
- 1 cup low-fat Greek yogurt
- 1 cup mixed berries (strawberries, blueberries, raspberries, etc.), fresh or frozen
- 1/2 cup honey or agave syrup
- 1 tablespoon lemon zest

Directions:

1. In a blender, combine the mixed berries, skim milk, Greek yogurt, honey or agave syrup, and lemon zest. Blend until the mixture is smooth and well combined.
2. Pour the berry mixture into the CREAMi Pint.
3. Freeze the pint for 24 hours.
4. After freezing, remove the lid from the CREAMi Pint and insert it into the Ninja CREAMi.
5. Select the 'Lite Ice Cream' function and process for 1.5 minutes.
6. Once processing is complete, add mix-ins or remove the ice cream from the pint.
7. Serve immediately for a soft-serve texture or transfer to a freezer-safe container for a firmer consistency if desired.

Nutritional Information (per serving): Protein: 8g | Carbohydrates: 35g | Sodium: 60mg | Potassium: 240mg | Sugar: 33g

Mango Tango Lite Ice Cream

Flavor profile: Juicy and sweet mangoes with a subtle hint of citrus, all wrapped in a creamy yet light ice cream base, delivering a tropical taste sensation.
Best for occasions: Summer Gatherings

❄️ Freeze time **24 hours**	🍲 Prep time **20 minutes**	⏰ Function time **1.5 minutes**	🕐 Servings **4**	🔥 Calories **120**	⚬ Complexity **Beginner**

Tags: Lite, Low Sugar, Fruity, Vegan   **Ninja CREAMi function:** Lite Ice Cream

Tools needed: Large bowl, Blender, Measuring cups, Measuring spoons, Ninja CREAMi

Ingredients:

- 2 cups skim milk
- 1 cup low-fat Greek yogurt
- 1 cup mango puree (fresh or canned)
- 1/2 cup sugar-free sweetener (like stevia or erythritol)
- 1 tablespoon lime juice
- 1 teaspoon vanilla extract

Directions:

1. In a blender, blend the mango puree, skim milk, Greek yogurt, sugar-free sweetener, lime juice, and vanilla extract until smooth.
2. Transfer the mixture to a large bowl.
3. Pour the mango mixture into the CREAMi Pint and freeze for 24 hours.
4. After freezing, remove the lid from the CREAMi Pint and insert it into the Ninja CREAMi.
5. Select the 'Lite Ice Cream' function and process for 1.5 minutes.
6. Once processing is complete, add mix-ins or remove the ice cream from the pint.
7. Serve immediately for a soft-serve texture, or transfer to a freezer-safe container for a firmer consistency if desired.

Nutritional Information (per serving): Protein: 6g | Carbohydrates: 18g | Sodium: 50mg | Potassium: 200mg | Sugar: 17g

---

Coffee Caramel Lite Ice Cream

Flavor profile: Robust and aromatic coffee paired with sweet, buttery caramel, all enveloped in a creamy, light ice cream base.
Best for occasions: Adults Only, Health-Conscious Gatherings

❄️ Freeze time **24 hours**	🍲 Prep time **15 minutes**	⏰ Function time **1.5 minutes**	🕐 Servings **4**	🔥 Calories **120**	⚬ Complexity **Intermediate**

Tags: Lite, Low Sugar, Vegan   **Ninja CREAMi function:** Lite Ice Cream

Tools needed: Large bowl, Whisk, Measuring cups, Measuring spoons, Ninja CREAMi

Ingredients:

- 2 cups skim milk
- 1 cup low-fat heavy cream
- 1/2 cup strong brewed coffee or espresso, cooled
- 1/2 cup sugar-free caramel syrup
- 1 tablespoon cream cheese, softened
- 1 teaspoon vanilla extract

Directions:

1. In a large bowl, whisk together the skim milk, low-fat heavy cream, cooled coffee or espresso, sugar-free caramel syrup, and vanilla extract until well combined.
2. Microwave the cream cheese for 10 seconds, then whisk it into the coffee mixture until smooth.
3. Pour the mixture into the CREAMi Pint and freeze for 24 hours.
4. After freezing, remove the lid from the CREAMi Pint and insert it into the Ninja CREAMi.
5. Select the 'Lite Ice Cream' function and process for 1.5 minutes.
6. Once processing is complete, add mix-ins or remove the ice cream from the pint.
7. Serve immediately for a soft texture or transfer to a freezer-safe container for a firmer consistency.

Nutritional Information (per serving): Protein: 4g | Carbohydrates: 18g | Sodium: 100mg | Potassium: 200mg | Sugar: 16g

Strawberry Coconut Dairy-Free Ice Cream

Flavor profile: A luscious mix of creamy coconut and vibrant strawberry flavors, creating a refreshing and naturally sweet treat.

Best for occasions: Summer Gatherings, Kids' Fun Day

| ❄️ Freeze time **24 hours** | 🍲 Prep time **20 minutes** | ⏰ Function time **1.5 minutes** | ⏲️ Servings **4** | 🔥 Calories **180** | Complexity **Beginner** |

Tags: Dairy Free, Vegan, Fruity, Sweet

Ninja CREAMi function: Ice Cream

Tools needed: Large bowl, Blender, Measuring cups, Measuring spoons, Ninja CREAMi

Ingredients:

- 1 cup coconut milk (full fat)
- 1 cup strawberries, fresh or frozen
- 1/2 cup agave syrup or maple syrup
- 1 teaspoon vanilla extract
- 1 tablespoon lime juice

Directions:

1. In a blender, blend the strawberries, coconut milk, agave or maple syrup, vanilla extract, and lime juice until smooth.
2. Transfer the blended mixture to a large bowl.
3. Pour the strawberry-coconut mixture into the CREAMi Pint and freeze for 24 hours.
4. After freezing, remove the lid from the CREAMi Pint and insert it into the Ninja CREAMi.
5. Select the 'Ice Cream' function and process for 1.5 minutes.
6. Once processing is complete, add mix-ins or remove the ice cream from the pint.
7. Serve immediately for a soft texture, or transfer to a freezer-safe container for a firmer consistency if desired.

Nutritional Information (per serving): Protein: 1g | Carbohydrates: 25g | Sodium: 10mg | Potassium: 200mg | Sugar: 24g

Chocolate Avocado Bliss Dairy-Free Ice Cream

Flavor profile: Creamy and subtly sweet, with the distinctive, smooth taste of avocado and a touch of vanilla, creating a luxurious and velvety texture.
Best for occasions: Health-Conscious Gatherings, Fancy Dinner Parties

❄ Freeze time **24 hours**	Prep time **20 minutes**	Function time **1.5 minutes**	Servings **4**	Calories **280**	Complexity **Intermediate**

Tags: Dairy Free, Vegan, Creamy, Sweet   **Ninja CREAMi function:** Ice Cream

Tools needed: Large bowl, Blender, Measuring cups, Measuring spoons, Ninja CREAMi

Ingredients:

- 2 ripe avocados, peeled and pitted
- 1 cup coconut milk (full fat)
- 1/2 cup agave syrup or maple syrup
- 1 teaspoon vanilla extract
- 2 tablespoons lime juice

Directions:

1. In a blender, puree the avocados, coconut milk, agave or maple syrup, vanilla extract, and lime juice until the mixture is smooth and creamy.
2. Transfer the pureed mixture into a large bowl.
3. Pour the avocado mixture into the CREAMi Pint and freeze for 24 hours.
4. After freezing, remove the lid from the CREAMi Pint and insert it into the Ninja CREAMi.
5. Select the 'Ice Cream' function and process for 1.5 minutes.
6. Once processing is complete, add mix-ins or remove the ice cream from the pint.
7. Serve immediately for a soft texture, or transfer to a freezer-safe container for a firmer consistency if desired.

Nutritional Information (per serving): Protein: 2g | Carbohydrates: 35g | Sodium: 15mg | Potassium: 500mg | Sugar: 32g

Coconut Lime Lite Ice Cream

Flavor profile: A creamy and tropical coconut base enhanced with a zesty, citrusy burst of lime, resulting in a refreshing and light ice cream experience.
Best for occasions: Summer Gatherings, Health-Conscious Gatherings

❄ Freeze time **24 hours**	Prep time **15 minutes**	Function time **1.5 minutes**	Servings **4**	Calories **100**	Complexity **Beginner**

Tags: Lite, Low Sugar, Vegan, Refreshing   **Ninja CREAMi function:** Lite Ice Cream

Tools needed: Large bowl, Whisk, Measuring cups, Measuring spoons, Ninja CREAMi

Ingredients:

- 2 cups light coconut milk
- 1/2 cup skim milk
- 1/2 cup sugar-free sweetener (like stevia or erythritol)
- 1 tablespoon cream cheese, softened
- 1 tablespoon lime zest
- 2 tablespoons lime juice
- 1 teaspoon vanilla extract

Directions:

1. In a large bowl, combine light coconut milk, skim milk, sugar-free sweetener, lime zest, lime juice, and vanilla extract. Whisk together until well blended.
2. Microwave the cream cheese for 10 seconds, then whisk into the mixture until smooth and no lumps remain.
3. Pour the mixture into the CREAMi Pint and freeze for 24 hours.
4. After freezing, remove the lid from the CREAMi Pint and insert it into the Ninja CREAMi.
5. Select the 'Lite Ice Cream' function and process for 1.5 minutes.
6. Once processing is complete, add mix-ins or remove the ice cream from the pint.
7. Serve immediately for a soft-serve texture or transfer to a freezer-safe container for a firmer consistency if desired.

Nutritional Information (per serving): Protein: 2g | Carbohydrates: 10g | Sodium: 40mg | Potassium: 150mg | Sugar: 9g

Blueberry Almond Swirl Dairy-Free Ice Cream

Flavor profile: The tangy and sweet taste of blueberries swirled with almond milk's subtle, creamy texture, complemented by vanilla.
Best for occasions: Health-Conscious Gatherings, Breakfast

❄ Freeze time	🍲 Prep time	⏰ Function time	🕑 Servings	🔥 Calories	Complexity
24 hours	**20 minutes**	**1.5 minutes**	**4**	**150**	**Intermediate**

Tags: Dairy Free, Vegan, Nutty, Fruity   **Ninja CREAMi function:** Ice Cream
Tools needed: Large bowl, Blender, Measuring cups, Measuring spoons, Ninja CREAMi

Ingredients:

- 2 cups almond milk
- 1 cup fresh or frozen blueberries
- 1/2 cup agave syrup or maple syrup
- 1 tablespoon almond butter
- 1 teaspoon vanilla extract
- 2 tablespoons blueberry jam (for swirl)

Directions:

1. In a blender, blend the almond milk, blueberries, agave or maple syrup, almond butter, and vanilla extract until smooth.
2. Transfer the mixture to a large bowl.
3. Pour the blueberry mixture into the CREAMi Pint and freeze for 24 hours.
4. After freezing, remove the lid from the CREAMi Pint and insert it into the Ninja CREAMi.
5. Select the 'Ice Cream' function and process for 1.5 minutes.
6. After processing, stir in the blueberry jam gently with a spoon to create a swirl effect. You may add more mix-ins or remove the ice cream from the pint.
7. Serve immediately for a soft texture, or transfer to a freezer-safe container for a firmer consistency if desired.

Nutritional Information (per serving): Protein: 1g | Carbohydrates: 30g | Sodium: 80mg | Potassium: 100mg | Sugar: 28g

Cinnamon Spiced Apple Dairy-Free Ice Cream

Flavor profile: Warm and cozy cinnamon spice with apple's sweet and tart notes in a rich, creamy, dairy-free base.
Best for occasions: Holiday Celebrations, Winter Comfort

❄️ **Freeze time** 24 hours	**Prep time** 25 minutes	**Function time** 1.5 minutes
Servings 4	**Calories** 160	**Complexity** **Intermediate**

Tags: Dairy Free, Vegan, Spiced, Sweet   **Ninja CREAMi function:** Ice Cream

Tools needed: Large bowl, Blender, Measuring cups, Measuring spoons, Ninja CREAMi

Ingredients:

- 2 cups almond milk
- 1 cup apple sauce or stewed apples
- 1/2 cup agave syrup or maple syrup
- 1 tablespoon ground cinnamon
- 1 teaspoon vanilla extract

Directions:

1. In a blender, blend the almond milk, apple sauce stewed apples, agave or maple syrup, ground cinnamon, and vanilla extract until smooth.
2. Transfer the mixture to a large bowl.
3. Pour the apple-cinnamon mixture into the CREAMi Pint and freeze for 24 hours.
4. After freezing, remove the lid from the CREAMi Pint and insert it into the Ninja CREAMi.
5. Select the 'Ice Cream' function and process for 1.5 minutes.
6. Once processing is complete, add mix-ins or remove the ice cream from the pint.
7. Serve immediately for a soft texture, or transfer to a freezer-safe container for a firmer consistency if desired.

Nutritional Information (per serving): Protein: 1g | Carbohydrates: 35g | Sodium: 80mg | Potassium: 100mg | Sugar: 33g

Classic Chocolate Fudge Milkshake

Flavor profile: Deep, rich chocolate harmoniously paired with smooth, creamy fudge, resulting in a velvety and intensely satisfying milkshake.
Best for occasions: Kids' Fun Day, Movie Night

Prep time **5 minutes**	Function time **1.5 minutes**	Servings **2**	Calories **380**	Complexity **Beginner**

Tags: Creamy, Sweet, Kid Friendly   *Ninja CREAMi function:* Milkshake

Tools needed: Ninja CREAMi, Measuring cups, Measuring spoons

Ingredients:

- 2 cups chocolate ice cream
- 1/4 cup chocolate fudge sauce
- 1/2 cup whole milk (or a non-dairy alternative for a dairy-free option)

Directions:

1. Add the chocolate ice cream to the Ninja CREAMi pint.
2. With a spoon, create a 1 ½ -inch wide hole reaching the pint's bottom. Add the chocolate fudge sauce to the hole in the pint.
3. Pour the milk over the ice cream and fudge sauce in the pint.
4. Insert the pint into the Ninja CREAMi.
5. Select the 'Milkshake' function and process for 1.5 minutes.
6. After processing, check the consistency. If you want your milkshake thinner, add 1–2 tablespoons of milk and select RE-SPIN. Process until the desired texture is achieved.
7. Pour the milkshake into glasses and serve immediately, optionally topped with whipped cream or a drizzle of chocolate sauce.

Nutritional Information (per serving): Protein: 6g | Carbohydrates: 55g | Sodium: 260mg | Potassium: 400mg | Sugar: 53g

Banana Nutella Milkshake

Flavor profile: Deep, rich chocolate harmoniously paired with smooth, creamy fudge, resulting in a velvety and intensely satisfying milkshake.
Best for occasions: Kids' Fun Day, Birthday Parties

Prep time **5 minutes**	Function time **1.5 minutes**	Servings **2**	Calories **380**	Complexity **Beginner**

Tags: Creamy, Nutty, Sweet, Kid Friendly   ***Ninja CREAMi function:*** Milkshake

Tools needed: Ninja CREAMi, Measuring cups, Measuring spoons

Ingredients:

- 2 cups chocolate ice cream
- 1/4 cup chocolate fudge sauce
- 1/2 cup whole milk (or a non-dairy alternative for a dairy-free option)

Directions:

1. Add the chocolate ice cream to the Ninja CREAMi pint.
2. With a spoon, create a 1 ½ -inch wide hole reaching the pint's bottom. Add the chocolate fudge sauce to the hole in the pint.
3. Pour the milk over the ice cream and fudge sauce in the pint.
4. Insert the pint into the Ninja CREAMi.
5. Select the 'Milkshake' function and process for 1.5 minutes.
6. After processing, check the consistency. If you want your milkshake thinner, add 1–2 tablespoons of milk and select RE-SPIN. Process until the desired texture is achieved.
7. Pour the milkshake into glasses and serve immediately, optionally topped with whipped cream or a drizzle of chocolate sauce.

Nutritional Information (per serving): Protein: 6g | Carbohydrates: 55g | Sodium: 260mg |Potassium: 400mg | Sugar: 53g |

Caramel Macchiato Milkshake

Flavor profile: Rich and robust coffee flavors beautifully intertwined with sweet, buttery caramel, all blended into a creamy, frothy milkshake.
Best for occasions: Movie Night, Adults Only

Prep time **5 minutes**	Function time **1.5 minutes**	Servings **2**	Calories **380**	Complexity **Beginner**

Tags: Creamy, Sweet, Coffee-flavored   ***Ninja CREAMi function:*** Milkshake

Tools needed: Ninja CREAMi, Measuring cups, Measuring spoons

Ingredients:

- 2 cups coffee or espresso-flavored ice cream
- 1/4 cup caramel sauce
- 1/2 cup cold brew coffee or strong brewed espresso, cooled
- 1/2 cup whole milk (or a non-dairy alternative for a dairy-free option)

Directions:

1. Add the coffee or espresso-flavored ice cream to the Ninja CREAMi pint.
2. With a spoon, create a 1 ½ -inch wide hole reaching the pint's bottom. Add the caramel sauce and cold brew coffee to the hole in the pint.
3. Pour the milk over the ice cream, caramel sauce, and coffee in the pint.
4. Insert the pint into the Ninja CREAMi.
5. Select the 'Milkshake' function and process for 1.5 minutes.
6. After processing, check the consistency. If you want your milkshake thinner, add 1–2 tablespoons of milk and select RE-SPIN. Process until the desired texture is achieved.
7. Pour the milkshake into glasses and serve immediately, optionally topped with whipped cream or a drizzle of caramel sauce.

Nutritional Information (per serving): Protein: 6g | Carbohydrates: 58g | Sodium: 220mg | Potassium: 400mg | Sugar: 52g

Cookies and Cream Milkshake

Flavor profile: Creamy and smooth vanilla ice cream mixed with the crunchy, chocolatey contrast of cookie pieces, creating a delightful and classic cookies and cream taste.
Best for occasions: Kids' Fun Day, Movie Night

Prep time **5 minutes**	Function time **1.5 minutes**	Servings **2**	Calories **350**	Complexity **Beginner**	

Tags: Creamy, Sweet, Kid Friendly   **Ninja CREAMi function:** Milkshake

Tools needed: Ninja CREAMi, Measuring cups, Measuring spoons

Ingredients:

- 2 cups cookies and cream ice cream
- 1/2 cup crushed Oreo cookies or similar chocolate sandwich cookies
- 1/2 cup whole milk (or a non-dairy alternative for a dairy-free option)

Directions:

1. Add the cookies and cream ice cream to the Ninja CREAMi pint.
2. With a spoon, create a 1½ -inch wide hole reaching the pint's bottom. Add the crushed Oreo cookies to the hole in the pint.
3. Pour the milk over the ice cream in the pint.
4. Insert the pint into the Ninja CREAMi.
5. Select the 'Milkshake' function and process for 1.5 minutes.
6. After processing, check the consistency. If you want your milkshake thinner, add 1–2 tablespoons of milk and select RE-SPIN. Process until the desired texture is achieved.
7. Pour the milkshake into glasses and serve immediately, optionally topped with whipped cream or additional crushed cookies.

Nutritional Information (per serving): Protein: 5g | Carbohydrates: 45g | Sodium: 280mg | Potassium: 300mg | Sugar: 40g

Blueberry Muffin Milkshake

Flavor profile: The sweet and tangy flavors of blueberries combined with the rich, buttery taste of muffin, all mixed into a creamy vanilla ice cream base, creating a milkshake that tastes like a blueberry muffin.
Best for occasions: Breakfast, Kids' Fun Day

Prep time **5 minutes**	Function time **1.5 minutes**	Servings **2**	Calories **360**	Complexity **Beginner**

Tags: Fruity, Sweet, Creamy   ***Ninja CREAMi function:*** Milkshake

Tools needed: Ninja CREAMi, Measuring cups, Measuring spoons

Ingredients:

- 2 cups vanilla ice cream
- 1/2 cup blueberries, fresh or frozen
- 1/2 cup crumbled blueberry muffin or muffin pieces
- 1/2 cup whole milk (or a non-dairy alternative for a dairy-free option)
- A pinch of cinnamon (optional)

Directions:

1. Add the vanilla ice cream to the Ninja CREAMi pint.
2. With a spoon, create a 1½ -inch wide hole reaching the pint's bottom. Add the blueberries and crumbled blueberry muffin pieces to the hole in the pint. Sprinkle with a pinch of cinnamon if desired.
3. Pour the milk over the ice cream.
4. Insert the pint into the Ninja CREAMi.
5. Select the 'Milkshake' function and process for 1.5 minutes.
6. After processing, check the consistency. If you want your milkshake thinner, add 1–2 tablespoons of milk and select RE-SPIN. Process until the desired texture is achieved.
7. Pour the milkshake into glasses and serve immediately, optionally garnished with additional blueberries or a small muffin piece.

Nutritional Information (per serving): Protein: 5g | Carbohydrates: 50g | Sodium: 220mg | Potassium: 350mg | Sugar: 45g

Strawberry Cheesecake Milkshake

Flavor profile: Creamy and rich cheesecake flavor fused with sweet and tangy strawberries, offering a perfect balance of fruitiness and indulgence.
Best for occasions: Romantic Occasions, Kids' Fun Day

Prep time **5 minutes**	Function time **1.5 minutes**	Servings **2**	Calories **380**	Complexity **Beginner**

Tags: Fruity, Sweet, Creamy   ***Ninja CREAMi function:*** Milkshake

Tools needed: Ninja CREAMi, Measuring cups, Measuring spoons

Ingredients:

- 2 cups strawberry ice cream
- 1/2 cup fresh strawberries, chopped
- 1/4 cup cream cheese, softened
- 1/4 cup graham cracker crumbs
- 1/2 cup whole milk (or a non-dairy alternative for a dairy-free option)

Directions:

1. Add the strawberry ice cream to the Ninja CREAMi pint.
2. With a spoon, create a 1½-inch wide hole reaching the pint's bottom. Add the chopped strawberries, cream cheese, and graham cracker crumbs to the hole in the pint.
3. Pour the milk over the ice cream.
4. Insert the pint into the Ninja CREAMi.
5. Select the 'Milkshake' function and process for 1.5 minutes.
6. After processing, check the consistency. If you want your milkshake thinner, add 1–2 tablespoons of milk and select RE-SPIN. Process until the desired texture is achieved.
7. Pour the milkshake into glasses and serve immediately, optionally garnished with a strawberry slice or a sprinkle of graham cracker crumbs.

Nutritional Information (per serving): Protein: 6g | Carbohydrates: 52g | Sodium: 280mg | Potassium: 370mg | Sugar: 47g

Key Lime Pie Milkshake

Flavor profile: A harmonious blend of tart key lime and sweet vanilla, combined with the richness of cream and the crunch of graham crackers, creates a delightful milkshake that mirrors the beloved pie.
Best for occasions: Summer Gatherings, Movie Night

Prep time **5 minutes**	Function time **1.5 minutes**	Servings **2**	Calories **360**	Complexity **Beginner**	

Tags: Tangy, Sweet, Creamy

Ninja CREAMi function: Milkshake

Tools needed: Ninja CREAMi, Measuring cups, Measuring spoonsc

Ingredients:

- 2 cups vanilla ice cream
- 1/4 cup key lime juice (fresh or bottled)
- Zest of 1 key lime (optional for added zing)
- 1/4 cup crushed graham crackers
- 1/2 cup whole milk (or a non-dairy alternative for a dairy-free option)
- Whipped cream (optional for topping)

Directions:

1. Add the vanilla ice cream to the Ninja CREAMi pint.
2. With a spoon, create a 1½-inch wide hole reaching the pint's bottom. Add the key lime juice, key lime zest, and crushed graham crackers to the hole in the pint.
3. Pour the milk over the ice cream.
4. Insert the pint into the Ninja CREAMi.
5. Select the 'Milkshake' function and process for 1.5 minutes.
6. After processing, check the consistency. If you want your milkshake thinner, add 1–2 tablespoons of milk and select RE-SPIN. Process until the desired texture is achieved.
7. Pour the milkshake into glasses, optionally topping with whipped cream and a sprinkle of graham cracker crumbs.

Nutritional Information (per serving): Protein: 5g | Carbohydrates: 50g | Sodium: 220mg | Potassium: 350mg | Sugar: 45g

Vegan Chocolate Peanut Butter Milkshake

Flavor profile: Rich and luscious chocolate perfectly paired with creamy, nutty peanut butter, offering a delightful balance of sweetness and depth in a smooth, vegan milkshake.

Prep time	Function time	Servings	Calories	Complexity
5 minutes	**1.5 minutes**	**2**	**380**	**Beginner**

Tags: Vegan, Nutty, Sweet, Creamy   ***Ninja CREAMi function:*** Milkshake

Tools needed: Ninja CREAMi, Measuring cups, Measuring spoons

Ingredients:

- 2 cups dairy-free chocolate ice cream
- 1/4 cup creamy peanut butter (ensure it's vegan)
- 1/2 cup almond milk or another non-dairy milk
- Vegan chocolate syrup (optional for drizzling)

Directions:

1. Add the dairy-free chocolate ice cream to the Ninja CREAMi pint.
2. With a spoon, create a 1½-inch wide hole reaching the pint's bottom. Add the creamy peanut butter to the hole in the pint.
3. Pour the almond milk over the ice cream in the pint.
4. Insert the pint into the Ninja CREAMi.
5. Select the 'Milkshake' function and process for 1.5 minutes.
6. After processing, check the consistency. If you want your milkshake thinner, add 1–2 tablespoons of milk and select RE-SPIN. Process until the desired texture is achieved.
7. Pour the milkshake into glasses and serve immediately, optionally drizzled with vegan chocolate syrup.

Nutritional Information (per serving): Protein: 8g | Carbohydrates: 45g | Sodium: 250mg | Potassium: 400mg | Sugar: 40g

---

Dairy-Free Oreo Milkshake

Flavor profile: A delightful combination of rich, chocolatey Oreo cookies and creamy, smooth vanilla, creating a classic and irresistible milkshake flavor that's dairy-free and delicious.

Best for occasions: Kids' Fun Day, Movie Night

Prep time	Function time	Servings	Calories	Complexity
5 minutes	**1.5 minutes**	**2**	**350**	**Beginner**

Tags: Dairy Free, Sweet, Creamy   ***Ninja CREAMi function:*** Milkshake

Tools needed: Ninja CREAMi, Measuring cups, Measuring spoons

Ingredients:

- 2 cups dairy-free vanilla ice cream
- 1/2 cup crushed dairy-free Oreo cookies or similar chocolate sandwich cookies
- 1/2 cup almond milk or another non-dairy milk

Directions:

1. Add the dairy-free vanilla ice cream to the Ninja CREAMi pint.
2. With a spoon, create a 1½-inch wide hole reaching the pint's bottom. Add the crushed dairy-free Oreo cookies to the hole in the pint.
3. Pour the non-dairy milk over the ice cream in the pint.
4. Insert the pint into the Ninja CREAMi.
5. Select the 'Milkshake' function and process for 1.5 minutes.
6. After processing, check the consistency. If you want your milkshake thinner, add 1–2 tablespoons of milk and select RE-SPIN. Process until the desired texture is achieved.
7. Pour the milkshake into glasses and serve immediately, optionally topped with additional crushed cookies or a dairy-free whipped cream.

Nutritional Information (per serving): Protein: 3g | Carbohydrates: 45g | Sodium: 260mg | Potassium: 200mg | Sugar: 40g

Piña Colada Milkshake

Flavor profile: A luscious blend of sweet pineapple and creamy coconut, enhanced with the smooth and warming notes of rum, offering a tropical and indulgent milkshake experience.
Best for occasions: Summer Gatherings, Romantic Occasions

Prep time **5 minutes**	Function time **1.5 minutes**	Servings **2**	Calories **360**	Complexity **Beginner**

Tags: Creamy, Sweet, Tropical, Adults Only   ***Ninja CREAMi function:*** Milkshake
Tools needed: Ninja CREAMi, Measuring cups, Measuring spoons

Ingredients:

- 2 cups coconut ice cream
- 1/2 cup pineapple chunks (fresh or canned)
- 1/4 cup coconut milk
- 2 tablespoons rum (white or spiced, based on preference)
- 1 tablespoon shredded coconut (optional for extra flavor)
- Pineapple slice and maraschino cherry (for garnish, optional)

Directions:

1. Add the coconut ice cream to the Ninja CREAMi pint.
2. With a spoon, create a 1½-inch wide hole reaching the pint's bottom. Add the pineapple chunks, shredded coconut, and rum to the hole in the pint.
3. Pour the coconut milk over the ice cream in the pint.
4. Insert the pint into the Ninja CREAMi.
5. Select the 'Milkshake' function and process for 1.5 minutes.
6. After processing, check the consistency. If you want your milkshake thinner, add 1–2 tablespoons of milk and select RE-SPIN. Process until the desired texture is achieved.
7. Pour the milkshake into glasses, optionally garnishing with a pineapple slice and a maraschino cherry.

Nutritional Information (per serving): Protein: 3g | Carbohydrates: 42g | Sodium: 120mg | Potassium: 250mg | Sugar: 45g

Mango Passion Fruit Sorbet

Flavor profile: Luscious and sweet mangoes balanced with passion fruit's tangy and slightly tart flavor, creating a tropical and refreshing sorbet with a perfect harmony of sweetness and acidity.
Best for occasions: Summer Gatherings, Romantic Occasions

❄ Freeze time **24 hours**	🍲 Prep time **15 minutes**	⏰ Function time **2 minutes**	🕐 Servings **4**	🔥 Calories **140**	〰 Complexity **Beginner**

Tags: Dairy Free, Gluten Free, Vegan, Refreshing, Sweet, Tangy, Fruity   ***Ninja CREAMi function:*** Sorbet
Tools needed: Ninja CREAMi, Measuring cups, Measuring spoons, Mixing bowl, Whisk

Ingredients:

- 2 cups mango puree
- Pulp of 3 passion fruits
- 1/2 cup granulated sugar
- 1 cup water
- 1 tablespoon lime juice

Directions:

1. In a mixing bowl, whisk together the mango puree, passion fruit pulp, granulated sugar, water, and lime juice until the sugar is fully dissolved and the mixture is well combined.
2. Pour the mixture into the Ninja CREAMi pint, ensuring it stays below the MAX FILL line.
3. Freeze the pint for 24 hours.
4. After freezing, remove the lid from the CREAMi Pint and insert it into the Ninja CREAMi.
5. Select the 'Sorbet' function and process for 2 minutes.
6. Serve the sorbet immediately, garnished with additional mango pieces or passion fruit seeds if desired.

Nutritional Information (per serving): Protein: 1g | Carbohydrates: 35g | Sodium: 10mg | Potassium: 180mg | Sugar: 34g

Raspberry Rose Sorbet

Flavor profile: Tangy and sweet raspberries delicately infused with the fragrant essence of rose water, creating a vibrant and sophisticated sorbet.
Best for occasions: Summer Gatherings, Health-Conscious Gatherings

❄ Freeze time **24 hours**	🍲 Prep time **15 minutes**	⏰ Function time **2 minutes**	🍕 Servings **4**	🔥 Calories **120**	⚬ Complexity **Beginner**

Tags: Dairy Free, Gluten Free, Refreshing, Sweet, Tangy, Floral, Fruity   *Ninja CREAMi function:* Sorbet
Tools needed: Ninja CREAMi, Measuring cups, Measuring spoons, Mixing bowl, Whisk

Ingredients:

- 3 cups fresh raspberries
- 1/2 cup granulated sugar
- 1 cup water
- 2 tablespoons rose water
- 1 tablespoon lemon juice

Directions:

1. In a mixing bowl, combine the fresh raspberries, sugar, water, and lemon juice. Use a whisk or a fork to press and stir the ingredients until the raspberries are well crushed, and the sugar is dissolved. Ensure the mixture is well combined.
2. Stir in the rose water.
3. Pour the raspberry and rose mixture into the Ninja CREAMi pint, ensuring it stays below the MAX FILL line.
4. Freeze the pint for 24 hours.
5. After freezing, remove the lid from the CREAMi Pint and insert it into the Ninja CREAMi.
6. Select the 'Sorbet' function and process for 2 minutes.
7. Serve the sorbet immediately, garnished with additional raspberries or a sprinkle of rose petals if desired.

Nutritional Information (per serving): Protein: 1g | Carbohydrates: 30g | Sodium: 5mg | Potassium: 115mg | Sugar: 29g

Blackberry Lavender Sorbet

Flavor profile: Juicy and tart blackberries combine with the delicate, fragrant essence of lavender, creating a refreshing and elegantly flavored sorbet.
Best for occasions: Fancy Dinner Parties, Health-Conscious Gatherings

❄ Freeze time **24 hours**	🍲 Prep time **15 minutes**	⏰ Function time **2 minutes**	🍕 Servings **4**	🔥 Calories **180**	⚬ Complexity **Beginner**

Tags: Dairy Free, Gluten Free, Vegan, Refreshing, Sweet, Floral, Fruity   *Ninja CREAMi function:* Sorbet
Tools needed: Ninja CREAMi, Measuring cups, Measuring spoons, Mixing bowl, Whisk

Ingredients:

- 3 cups blackberries, fresh or thawed from frozen
- 1 cup granulated sugar
- 1 1/2 cups water
- 1 tablespoon dried lavender flowers (culinary grade)
- 2 tablespoons lemon juice

Directions:

1. In a mixing bowl, combine the blackberries, sugar, water, and lemon juice. Use a whisk or a fork to crush the blackberries and mix until the sugar is dissolved.
2. Stir in the dried lavender flowers.
3. Let the mixture sit for about 10 minutes to infuse the lavender flavor, then strain the mixture to remove the lavender and blackberry seeds.
4. Pour the strained mixture into the Ninja CREAMi pint, ensuring it stays below the MAX FILL line.
5. Freeze the pint for 24 hours.
6. After freezing, remove the lid from the CREAMi Pint and insert it into the Ninja CREAMi.
7. Select the 'Sorbet' function and process for 2 minutes.
8. Serve the sorbet immediately, optionally garnished with fresh blackberries or a sprig of lavender.

Nutritional Information (per serving): Protein: 1g | Carbohydrates: 45g | Sodium: 5mg | Potassium: 140mg | Sugar: 44g

Watermelon Mint Sorbet

Flavor profile: The sweet, hydrating taste of ripe watermelon combined with the fresh, invigorating notes of mint creates a vibrant and cooling sorbet.

Best for occasions: Summer Gatherings, Kids' Fun Day

❄️ Freeze time **24 hours**	🍳 Prep time **15 minutes**	⏰ Function time **2 minutes**	⏱️ Servings **4**	🔥 Calories **120**	〰️ Complexity **Beginner**

Tags: Dairy Free, Gluten Free, Vegan, Refreshing, Sweet, Herbal, Fruity ⬥ ***Ninja CREAMi function:*** Sorbet

Tools needed: Ninja CREAMi, Measuring cups, Measuring spoons, Mixing bowl, Whisk

Ingredients:

- 4 cups watermelon, cubed and seeds removed
- 1/2 cup granulated sugar
- 1 cup water
- 1/4 cup fresh mint leaves, finely chopped
- 2 tablespoons lime juice

Directions:

1. In a mixing bowl, combine the watermelon cubes, granulated sugar, water, and lime juice. Use a whisk or a fork to gently crush the watermelon and mix until the sugar is dissolved.
2. Stir in the finely chopped mint leaves, ensuring they are well incorporated into the mixture.
3. Pour the watermelon and mint mixture into the Ninja CREAMi pint, ensuring it stays below the MAX FILL line.
4. Freeze the pint for 24 hours.
5. After freezing, remove the lid from the CREAMi Pint and insert it into the Ninja CREAMi.
6. Select the 'Sorbet' function and process for 2 minutes.
7. Serve the sorbet immediately, optionally garnished with additional mint leaves or small watermelon wedges.

Nutritional Information (per serving): Protein: 1g | Carbohydrates: 30g | Sodium: 5mg | Potassium: 170mg | Sugar: 29g

Kiwi Honeydew Sorbet

Flavor profile: A delightful combination of tangy kiwi and sweet, juicy honeydew melon, creating a refreshing and invigorating vibrant and delicately balanced sorbet.
Best for occasions: Kids' Fun Day, Summer Gatherings

Freeze time	Prep time	Function time	Servings	Calories	Complexity
24 hours	15 minutes	2 minutes	4	140	Beginner

Tags: Dairy Free, Gluten Free, Vegetarian, Refreshing, Sweet, Tangy, Fruity   *Ninja CREAMi function:* Sorbet
Tools needed: Ninja CREAMi, Measuring cups, Measuring spoons, Mixing bowl, Whisk

Ingredients:

- 2 cups honeydew melon, cubed
- 2 cups kiwi, peeled and sliced
- 1/2 cup granulated sugar
- 1 cup water
- 2 tablespoons lime juice

Directions:

1. In a mixing bowl, combine the honeydew melon, kiwi, granulated sugar, water, and lime juice. Use a whisk or a fork to gently crush the fruits and stir until the sugar is dissolved and the mixture is well combined.
2. Pour the fruit mixture into the Ninja CREAMi pint, ensuring it stays below the MAX FILL line.
3. Freeze the pint for 24 hours.
4. After freezing, remove the lid from the CREAMi Pint and insert it into the Ninja CREAMi.
5. Select the 'Sorbet' function and process for 2 minutes.
6. Serve the sorbet immediately, optionally garnished with additional kiwi or honeydew melon slices.

Nutritional Information (per serving): Protein: 1g | Carbohydrates: 35g | Sodium: 10mg | Potassium: 250mg | Sugar: 34g

---

Coconut Lime Sorbet

Flavor profile: The luxurious and creamy taste of coconut combined with the fresh, citrusy zest of lime creates a refreshing and smooth sorbet.
Best for occasions: Health-Conscious Gatherings, Summer Gatherings

Freeze time	Prep time	Function time	Servings	Calories	Complexity
24 hours	15 minutes	2 minutes	4	180	Beginner

Tags: Dairy Free, Refreshing, Creamy, Tangy   *Ninja CREAMi function:* Sorbet
Tools needed: Ninja CREAMi, Measuring cups, Measuring spoons, Mixing bowl, Whisk

Ingredients:

- 2 cups coconut milk (canned, full-fat for best texture)
- 1/2 cup granulated sugar
- 1 cup water
- 1/4 cup lime juice (freshly squeezed)
- Zest of 2 limes

Directions:

1. In a mixing bowl, combine the coconut milk, granulated sugar, water, lime juice, and lime zest. Stir, whisk, or press the mixture until the sugar is dissolved and everything is well combined.
2. Pour the coconut lime mixture into the Ninja CREAMi pint, ensuring it stays below the MAX FILL line.
3. Freeze the pint for 24 hours.
4. After freezing, remove the lid from the CREAMi Pint and insert it into the Ninja CREAMi.
5. Select the 'Sorbet' function and process for 2 minutes.
6. Serve the sorbet immediately, optionally garnished with additional lime zest or coconut flakes.

Nutritional Information (per serving): Protein: 1g | Carbohydrates: 20g | Sodium: 15mg | Potassium: 180mg | Sugar: 19g

Pear Ginger Sorbet

Flavor profile: The natural sweetness of juicy pears is beautifully complemented by fresh ginger's warm, spicy notes, creating soothing and refreshing sorbets.
Best for occasions: Health-Conscious Gatherings, Fancy Dinner Parties

❄ Freeze time **24 hours**	🍲 Prep time **20 minutes**	⏰ Function time **2 minutes**	⏲ Servings **4**	🔥 Calories **150**	➝ Complexity **Beginner**

Tags: Dairy Free, Gluten Free, Vegetarian, Refreshing, Sweet, Spiced, Fruity   ***Ninja CREAMi function:*** Sorbet
Tools needed: Ninja CREAMi, Measuring cups, Measuring spoons, Mixing bowl, Whisk

Ingredients:

- 4 cups pear puree (from ripe pears)
- 1/2 cup granulated sugar
- 1 cup water
- 2 tablespoons fresh ginger, finely grated
- 2 tablespoons lemon juice

Directions:

1. In a mixing bowl, combine the pear puree, granulated sugar, water, and lemon juice. Stir well until the sugar is completely dissolved.
2. Add the finely grated ginger to the mixture, thoroughly combining it.
3. Pour the pear and ginger mixture into the Ninja CREAMi pint, ensuring it stays below the MAX FILL line.
4. Freeze the pint for 24 hours.
5. After freezing, remove the lid from the CREAMi Pint and insert it into the Ninja CREAMi.
6. Select the 'Sorbet' function and process for 2 minutes.
7. Serve the sorbet immediately, optionally garnished with a thin pear slice or a grated ginger sprinkle.

Nutritional Information (per serving): Protein: 0.5g | Carbohydrates: 38g | Sodium: 10mg | Potassium: 120mg | Sugar: 37g

Cherry Almond Sorbet

Flavor profile: Luscious and sweet cherries paired with the subtle, nutty notes of almond extract create a sorbet that is deep in flavor and wonderfully fragrant.
Best for occasions: Romantic Occasions, Summer Gatherings

❄️ Freeze time **24 hours**	Prep time **20 minutes**	Function time **2 minutes**	Servings **4**	Calories **160**	Complexity **Beginner**

Tags: Dairy Free, Gluten Free, Vegan, Low Sugar, Vegetarian, Refreshing, Sweet, Nutty, Fruity

Ninja CREAMi function: Sorbet

Tools needed: Ninja CREAMi, Measuring cups, Measuring spoons, Mixing bowl, Whisk

Ingredients:

- 3 cups canned cherries in light syrup (drained)
- 1/2 cup granulated sugar
- 1 cup water
- 1 tablespoon almond extract
- 1 tablespoon lemon juice

Directions:

1. In a mixing bowl, combine the drained canned cherries, granulated sugar, water, almond extract, and lemon juice. Use a whisk or a fork to gently crush the cherries and mix until the sugar is dissolved.
2. Pour the cherry and almond mixture into the Ninja CREAMi pint, ensuring it stays below the MAX FILL line.
3. Freeze the pint for 24 hours.
4. After freezing, remove the lid from the CREAMi Pint and insert it into the Ninja CREAMi.
5. Select the 'Sorbet' function and process for 2 minutes.
6. Serve the sorbet immediately, optionally garnished with a few whole cherries or a sprinkle of sliced almonds.

Nutritional Information (per serving): Protein: 1g | Carbohydrates: 38g | Sodium: 5mg | Potassium: 180mg | Sugar: 37g

---

Mojito Lime Sorbet

Flavor profile: A vibrant blend of tart lime and fresh mint, enhanced with the subtle warmth of rum, resulting in an exhilarating and soothing sorbet.
Best for occasions: Adults Only, Summer Gatherings

❄️ Freeze time **24 hours**	Prep time **20 minutes**	Function time **2 minutes**	Servings **4**	Calories **180**	Complexity **Beginner**

Tags: Dairy Free, Low Sugar, Adults Only, Refreshing, Sweet, Tangy, Herbal

Ninja CREAMi function: Sorbet

Tools needed: Ninja CREAMi, Measuring cups, Measuring spoons, Mixing bowl, Whisk

Ingredients:

- 1/2 cup fresh lime juice
- 1/2 cup white rum
- 1 cup granulated sugar
- 1 1/2 cups water
- 1/4 cup fresh mint leaves, finely chopped
- Zest of 2 limes

Directions:

1. In a mixing bowl, combine the lime juice, white rum, granulated sugar, water, and lime zest. Stir well until the sugar is completely dissolved.
2. Add the finely chopped mint leaves to the mixture, ensuring they are well incorporated.
3. Pour the mojito mixture into the Ninja CREAMi pint, ensuring it stays below the MAX FILL line.
4. Freeze the pint for 24 hours.
5. After freezing, remove the lid from the CREAMi Pint and insert it into the Ninja CREAMi.
6. Select the 'Sorbet' function and process for 2 minutes.
7. Serve the sorbet immediately, optionally garnished with additional mint leaves or a lime wedge.

Nutritional Information (per serving): Protein: 0g | Carbohydrates: 28g | Sodium: 5mg | Potassium: 40mg | Sugar: 27g

Raspberry White Chocolate Gelato

Flavor profile: The vibrant, tangy taste of fresh raspberries melds beautifully with the smooth, sweet notes of white chocolate, creating a harmonious and indulgent gelato experience.
Best for occasions: Romantic Occasions, Health-Conscious Gatherings

❄ Freeze time **24 hours**	Prep time **30 minutes**	⏰ Function time **7-10 minutes**	Servings **4**	Calories **440**	Complexity **Intermediate**

Tags: Creamy, Sweet, Fruity

Ninja CREAMi function: Gelato

Tools needed: Ninja CREAMi, Saucepan, Whisk, Measuring cups, Measuring spoons, Large bowl

Ingredients:

- 1 cup whole milk
- 1 cup heavy cream
- 1/2 cup granulated sugar
- 4 egg yolks
- 1 cup raspberries, fresh or frozen
- 1/2 cup white chocolate chips
- 1 teaspoon lemon juice

Directions:

1. In a saucepan, heat the milk, heavy cream, and sugar over medium heat until it begins to simmer. Remove from heat.
2. In a large bowl, whisk the egg yolks until they become pale and fluffy.
3. Gradually whisk the hot milk mixture into the egg yolks to temper them.
4. Return the mixture to the saucepan and cook over low heat, stirring continuously, until the mixture thickens enough to coat the back of a spoon.
5. Remove from heat. Mash the raspberries with lemon juice and strain them to remove seeds. Stir the raspberry puree into the custard mixture. Allow the mixture to cool, then stir in the white chocolate chips until evenly distributed.
6. Pour the mixture into the Ninja CREAMi pint.
7. Freeze the pint for 24 hours. After freezing, remove the lid from the CREAMi Pint and insert it into the Ninja CREAMi.
8. Select the 'Gelato' function and process for 7-10 minutes.
9. Serve the gelato immediately for a soft texture, or place it in the freezer for 1-2 hours for a firmer consistency.

Nutritional Information (per serving): Protein: 6g | Carbohydrates: 40g | Sodium: 70mg | Potassium: 210mg | Sugar: 39g

Lemon Custard Gelato

Flavor profile: The bright, tangy zest of lemon is perfectly infused into a rich and creamy custard base, creating a refreshing and satisfyingly smooth gela

Best for occasions: Summer Gatherings, Health-Conscious Gatherings

| ❄ Freeze time **24 hours** | 🍲 Prep time **30 minutes** | ⏰ Function time **7-10 minutes** | Servings **4** | Calories **350** | Complexity **Beginner** |

Tags: Vegetarian, Refreshing, Creamy, Sweet, Tangy   **Ninja CREAMi function:** Gelato

Tools needed: Ninja CREAMi, Saucepan, Whisk, Measuring cups, Measuring spoons, Large bowl

Ingredients:

- 1 cup whole milk
- 1 cup heavy cream
- 3/4 cup granulated sugar
- 5 egg yolks
- Zest of 3 lemons
- 1/4 cup fresh lemon juice

Directions:

1. In a saucepan, combine the milk, heavy cream, and lemon zest. Heat over medium heat until it starts to simmer, then remove from the heat.
2. In a large bowl, whisk together the egg yolks and sugar until they turn light and fluffy. Gradually add the warm milk mixture to the egg yolks, whisking constantly to temper the eggs.
3. Return the mixture to the saucepan and heat over low heat. Stir continuously until the mixture thickens enough to coat the back of a spoon.
4. Remove from heat and let it cool. Once cooled, stir in the lemon juice.
5. Pour the mixture into the Ninja CREAMi pint.
6. Freeze the pint for 24 hours.
7. After freezing, remove the lid from the CREAMi Pint and insert it into the Ninja CREAMi.
8. Select the 'Gelato' function and process for 7-10 minutes.
9. Serve the gelato immediately for a soft consistency, or store it in the freezer for a few hours for a firmer texture.

Nutritional Information (per serving): Protein: 5g | Carbohydrates: 32g | Sodium: 55mg | Potassium: 150mg | Sugar: 31

Banana Peanut Dairy-free Gelato

Flavor profile: The smooth and velvety texture of ripe bananas provides a naturally sweet base, complemented by the hearty and rich flavor of peanut butter, creating a nourishing and indulgent gelato.

Best for occasions: Health-Conscious Gatherings, Kids' Fun Day

| ❄ Freeze time **24 hours** | 🍲 Prep time **20 minutes** | ⏰ Function time **7-10 minutes** | Servings **4** | Calories **280** | Complexity **Beginner** |

Tags: Dairy Free, Vegan, Creamy, Sweet, Nutty   **Ninja CREAMi function:** Gelato

Tools needed: Ninja CREAMi, Blender or food processor, Measuring cups, Measuring spoons, Large bowl

Ingredients:

- 1 cup almond milk or other non-dairy milk
- 2 ripe bananas, sliced and frozen
- 1/2 cup natural peanut butter
- 1/4 cup maple syrup or agave nectar
- 1 teaspoon vanilla extract

Directions:

1. In a blender or food processor, blend the frozen banana slices until they reach a smooth and creamy consistency.
2. Add peanut butter, almond milk, maple syrup, agave nectar, and vanilla extract to the blended bananas. Blend again until all ingredients are well combined, and the mixture is smooth.
3. Pour the mixture into the Ninja CREAMi pint.
4. Freeze the pint for 24 hours.
5. After freezing, remove the lid from the CREAMi Pint and insert it into the Ninja CREAMi.
6. Select the 'Gelato' function and process for 7-10 minutes.
7. Serve the gelato immediately for a soft texture, or transfer to a freezer-safe container and freeze for an additional 1-2 hours for a firmer consistency.

Nutritional Information (per serving): Protein: 7g | Carbohydrates: 35g | Sodium: 150mg | Potassium: 400mg | Sugar: 34g

Berry Bliss Lite Gelato

Flavor profile: A luscious blend of various berries, each contributing its unique sweet and tart notes, creates a symphony of flavors. This gelato is a treat for your taste buds and a visual delight with its rich, natural colors.
Best for occasions: Health-Conscious Gatherings, Breakfast

❄️ Freeze time **24 hours**	🍲 Prep time **30 minutes**	⏰ Function time **7-10 minutes**	🕐 Servings **4**	🔥 Calories **220**	⚊ Complexity **Beginner**

Tags: Lite, Vegetarian, Creamy, Sweet, Fruity   **Ninja CREAMi function:** Gelato

Tools needed: Ninja CREAMi, Saucepan, Whisk, Measuring cups, Measuring spoons, Large bowl, Blender or food processor

Ingredients:

- 1 cup skim milk
- 1 cup light cream or half-and-half
- 1/2 cup granulated sugar or sugar substitute
- 4 egg yolks
- 2 cups mixed berries (such as strawberries, blueberries, and raspberries), fresh or frozen
- 1 teaspoon vanilla extract

Directions:

1. In a blender or food processor, puree the mixed berries until smooth. Strain to remove seeds if desired.
2. In a saucepan, heat the skim milk and light cream over medium heat until it begins to simmer. Remove from heat.
3. In a large bowl, whisk the egg yolks and sugar (or sugar substitute) until light and fluffy. Gradually whisk the hot milk mixture into the egg yolks to temper them.
4. Return the mixture to the saucepan and cook over low heat, stirring continuously, until the mixture thickens slightly and coats the back of a spoon.
5. Remove from heat and let the mixture cool. Stir in the berry puree and vanilla extract. Pour the mixture into the Ninja CREAMi pint.
6. Freeze the pint for 24 hours.
7. After freezing, remove the lid from the CREAMi Pint and insert it into the Ninja CREAMi.
8. Select the 'Gelato' function and process for 7-10 minutes.
9. Serve immediately for a soft texture, or transfer to a freezer-safe container and freeze for an additional 1-2 hours for a firmer consistency.

Nutritional Information (per serving): Protein: 6g | Carbohydrates: 30g | Sodium: 70mg | Potassium: 200mg | Sugar: 28g

Biscotti Gelato

Flavor profile: This gelato features a creamy, sweet base enhanced by the rich flavor of almonds, reminiscent of traditional biscotti. The added crunch from the biscotti pieces provides a delightful contrast, making each bite both satisfying and luxurious.
Best for occasions: Breakfast, Fancy Dinner Parties

❄ Freeze time **24 hours**	⏲ Prep time **35 minutes**	⏰ Function time **7-10 minutes for Gelato, + 1.5 minutes Mix-in time**	Servings **4**	Calories **370**	Complexity **Beginner**

Tags: Vegetarian, Creamy, Sweet, Nutty   *Ninja CREAMi function:* Gelato, Mix-in

Tools needed: Ninja CREAMi, Saucepan, Whisk, Measuring cups, Measuring spoons, Large bowl

Ingredients:

- 1 cup whole milk
- 1 cup heavy cream
- 1/2 cup granulated sugar
- 4 egg yolks
- 1 teaspoon almond extract
- 1/2 cup crushed almond biscotti (for mix-in)

Directions:

1. In a saucepan, combine milk, heavy cream, and sugar. Heat over medium until it begins to simmer, then remove from heat.
2. In a large bowl, whisk egg yolks until light. Gradually whisk in the hot milk mixture to temper the yolks. Return the mixture to the saucepan. Cook over low heat, stirring, until it thickens enough to coat a spoon.
3. Remove from heat, stir in almond extract, and let cool.
4. Pour the mixture into the Ninja CREAMi pint and freeze for 24 hours.
5. After freezing, remove the lid from the CREAMi Pint and insert it into the Ninja CREAMi. Select the 'Gelato' function and process for 7-10 minutes.
6. After processing, open the lid. With a spoon, create a 1½-inch wide hole in the bottom of the pint. Add the crushed biscotti into the hole.
7. Replace the lid and select the 'Mix-in' function to blend the biscotti into the gelato. Serve immediately for a soft texture, or freeze for 1-2 hours for a firmer consistency.

Nutritional Information (per serving): Protein: 6g | Carbohydrates: 32g | Sodium: 80mg | Potassium: 230mg | Sugar: 31g

---

Peach and Prosecco Gelato

Flavor profile: Juicy, ripe peaches provide a natural sweetness and fruity aroma, beautifully complemented by the crisp, refreshing notes of Prosecco. Together, they create a gelato that's both vibrant and indulgent, with a subtle alcoholic kick.
Best for occasions: Fancy Dinner Parties, Summer Gatherings

❄ Freeze time **24 hours**	⏲ Prep time **30 minutes**	⏰ Function time **7-10 minutes**	Servings **4**	Calories **320**	Complexity **Beginner**

Tags: Adults Only, Creamy, Sweet, Tangy, Fruity   *Ninja CREAMi function:* Gelato

Tools needed: Ninja CREAMi, Saucepan, Blender or food processor, Whisk, Measuring cups, Measuring spoons, Large bowl

Ingredients:

- 1 cup whole milk
- 1 cup heavy cream
- 1/2 cup granulated sugar
- 4 egg yolks
- 2 ripe peaches, peeled and diced
- 1/2 cup Prosecco
- 1 teaspoon lemon juice
- 1 teaspoon vanilla extract

Directions:

1. In a blender or food processor, puree the diced peaches until smooth.
2. In a saucepan, heat the milk, heavy cream, and sugar over medium heat until it begins to simmer. Remove from heat.
3. In a large bowl, whisk the egg yolks until they become pale and fluffy.
4. Gradually whisk the hot milk mixture into the egg yolks to temper them. Return the mixture to the saucepan and cook over low heat, stirring continuously, until the mixture thickens slightly and coats the back of a spoon.
5. Remove from heat and let the mixture cool. Stir in the peach puree, Prosecco, lemon juice, and vanilla extract. Pour the mixture into the Ninja CREAMi pint. Freeze the pint for 24 hours.
6. After freezing, remove the lid from the CREAMi Pint and insert it into the Ninja CREAMi. Select the 'Gelato' function and process for 7-10 min.
7. Serve immediately for a soft texture, or transfer to a freezer-safe container and freeze for an additional 1-2 hours for a firmer consistency.

Nutritional Information (per serving): Protein: 4g | Carbohydrates: 25g | Sodium: 55mg | Potassium: 210mg | Sugar: 24g

Orange Blossom Gelato

Flavor profile: A delightful blend of sweet and floral orange blossom paired with the tangy zest of fresh oranges, creating a fragrant and refreshingly citrusy gelato.

Best for occasions: Fancy Dinner Parties, Summer Gatherings

❄️ Freeze time **24 hours**	🍲 Prep time **30 minutes**	⏰ Function time **7-10 minutes**	⏱️ Servings **4**	🔥 Calories **350**	📊 Complexity **Beginner**

Tags: Vegetarian, Refreshing, Creamy, Sweet, Tangy, Floral   **Ninja CREAMi function:** Gelato

Tools needed: Ninja CREAMi, Saucepan, Whisk, Measuring cups, Measuring spoons, Large bowl

Ingredients:

- 1 cup whole milk
- 1 cup heavy cream
- 3/4 cup granulated sugar
- 4 egg yolks
- Zest of 2 oranges
- 1/4 cup fresh orange juice
- 2 tablespoons orange blossom water

Directions:

1. In a saucepan, combine the milk, heavy cream, and orange zest. Heat over medium heat until it begins to simmer, then remove from heat.
2. In a large bowl, whisk the egg yolks and sugar until light and fluffy.
3. Gradually whisk the hot milk mixture into the egg yolks to temper them.
4. Return the mixture to the saucepan and cook over low heat, stirring constantly, until it thickens slightly and coats the back of a spoon.
5. Remove from heat and let the mixture cool. Stir in the orange juice and orange blossom water.
6. Pour the mixture into the Ninja CREAMi pint.
7. Freeze the pint for 24 hours.
8. After freezing, remove the lid from the CREAMi Pint and insert it into the Ninja CREAMi.
9. Select the 'Gelato' function and process for 7-10 minutes.
10. Serve immediately for a soft consistency, or place in the freezer for 1-2 hours for a firmer texture.

Nutritional Information (per serving): Protein: 5g | Carbohydrates: 30g | Sodium: 50mg | Potassium: 180mg | Sugar: 29g

Mint Chocolate Chip Gelato

Flavor profile: The gelato features a fresh, minty base with a hint of sweetness, perfectly complemented by decadent chocolate chips. Mix-ins add a delightful crunch, making each bite a perfect balance of creamy and crispy textures.
Best for occasions: Kids' Fun Day, Summer Gatherings

| ❄️ Freeze time
24 hours | Prep time
35 minutes | Function time
**7-10 minutes for Gelato,
1.5 minutes for mix-ins** | Servings
4 | Calories
360 | Complexity
Intermediate |

Tags: Vegetarian, Refreshing, Creamy, Sweet   **Ninja CREAMi function:** Gelato, Mix-in

Tools needed: Ninja CREAMi, Saucepan, Whisk, Measuring cups, Measuring spoons, Large bowl

Ingredients:

- 1 cup whole milk
- 1 cup heavy cream
- 1/2 cup granulated sugar
- 4 egg yolks
- 1 teaspoon peppermint extract
- 1/2 cup mini chocolate chips (for mix-ins)
- Additional mini chocolate chips for garnish (optional)

Directions:

1. In a saucepan, combine the milk, heavy cream, and sugar. Heat over medium heat until it begins to simmer, then remove from heat.
2. In a large bowl, whisk the egg yolks until light and fluffy. Gradually whisk the hot milk mixture into the egg yolks to temper them.
3. Return the mixture to the saucepan and cook over low heat, stirring continuously, until it thickens enough to coat the back of a spoon.
4. Remove from heat and let the mixture cool. Stir in the peppermint extract. Pour the mixture into the Ninja CREAMi pint.
5. Freeze the pint for 24 hours. After freezing, remove the lid from the CREAMi Pint and insert it into the Ninja CREAMi.
6. Select the 'Gelato' function and process for 7-10 minutes.
7. Pause the process and open the lid. With a spoon, create a 1½-inch wide hole reaching the pint's bottom. Add the mini chocolate chips into this hole.
8. Replace the lid and select the 'Mix-in' function. Process for 1.5 minutes to blend the chocolate chips into the gelato.
9. Serve immediately for a soft texture, or transfer to a freezer-safe container and freeze for 1-2 hours for a firmer consistency. Garnish with additional mini chocolate chips if desired.

Nutritional Information (per serving): Protein: 6g | Carbohydrates: 32g | Sodium: 80mg | Potassium: 220mg | Sugar: 30g

Tropical Sunrise Bowl

Flavor profile: Sweet and tropical with a creamy, fruity essence.
Best for occasions: Breakfast, Health-Conscious Gatherings

❄ Freeze time **24 hours**	Prep time **10 minutes**	Function time **2 minutes**	Servings **4**	Calories **180**	Complexity **Beginner**

Tags: Vegetarian, Refreshing, Creamy, Sweet, Fruity   **Ninja CREAMi function:** Smoothie Bowl
Tools needed: Ninja CREAMi, CREAMi Pint, Large Bowl, Spoon, Measuring Cups, Measuring Spoons

Ingredients:

- 2 cups frozen mango chunks
- 1 cup frozen pineapple pieces
- 1 ripe banana
- 1/2 cup coconut milk
- 2 tablespoons vanilla protein powder
- 1/4 cup water or additional coconut milk for consistency

Directions:

1. In a large bowl, combine the frozen mango chunks, pineapple pieces, sliced banana, coconut milk, and vanilla protein powder.
2. Mix water or coconut milk well to achieve a slightly fluid yet thick consistency.
3. Pour the mixture into the CREAMi Pint up to the MAX Fill line.
4. Secure the CREAMi Pint lid and freeze for 24 hours.
5. After freezing, remove the CREAMi Pint lid and insert the pint into the Ninja CREAMi.
6. Use the 'Smoothie Bowl' function to process the mixture until it is creamy.
7. Serve immediately, optionally topped with shredded coconut, sliced kiwi, or chia seeds.

Nutritional Information (per serving): Protein: 4g | Carbohydrates: 33g | Sodium: 20mg | Potassium: 300mg | Sugar: 32g

Raspberry Lemonade Bowl

Flavor profile: A delightful mix of sweet and tart with a zesty lemon wedge.
Best for occasions: Breakfast, Summer Gatherings

❄ Freeze time **24 hours**	Prep time **10 minutes**	⏰ Function time **2 minutes**	Servings **4**	Calories **160**	Complexity **Beginner**

Tags: Vegetarian, Refreshing, Sweet, Tangy   ***Ninja CREAMi function:*** Smoothie Bowl

Tools needed: Ninja CREAMi, CREAMi Pint, Large Bowl, Spoon, Measuring Cups, Measuring Spoons

Ingredients:

- 2 cups frozen raspberries
- 1 banana, sliced
- 1/2 cup Greek yogurt
- 4 tablespoons honey or agave syrup
- Juice and zest from 2 lemons
- 1/4 cup water or coconut water, as needed for consistency

Directions:

1. In a large bowl, mix the frozen raspberries, sliced banana, Greek yogurt, honey, lemon juice, and half of the lemon zest.
2. Gradually pour in the water or coconut water, stirring until the mixture is slightly thinner than a traditional smoothie consistency.
3. Transfer the mixture into the CREAMi Pint, filling it to the MAX Fill line.
4. Secure the lid on the CREAMi Pint and freeze for 24 hours.
5. Once frozen, remove the lid from the CREAMi Pint and place the pint into the Ninja CREAMi.
6. Process using the 'Smoothie Bowl' function until the mixture reaches a smooth, creamy texture.
7. Serve the smoothie bowl immediately, garnished with the remaining lemon zest or additional raspberries if desired.

Nutritional Information (per serving): Protein: 3g | Carbohydrates: 36g | Sodium: 15mg | Potassium: 210mg | Sugar: 35g

Peanut Butter Dream Bowl

Flavor profile: Rich and creamy with a deep peanut butter taste, complemented by sweet banana and a hint of chocolate.
Best for occasions: Health-Conscious Gatherings, Breakfast

❄ Freeze time **24 hours**	Prep time **10 minutes**	⏰ Function time **2 minutes**	Servings **4**	Calories **330**	Complexity **Beginner**

Tags: Vegetarian, Refreshing, Creamy, Spiced, Sweet, Nutty   ***Ninja CREAMi function:*** Smoothie Bowl

Tools needed: Ninja CREAMi, CREAMi Pint, Large Bowl, Spoon, Measuring Cups, Measuring Spoons

Ingredients:

- 2 ripe bananas, sliced and frozen
- 1/2 cup peanut butter
- 2 tablespoons cocoa powder
- 1 cup Greek yogurt
- 1/4 cup almond milk
- 2 tablespoons honey or maple syrup (optional)
- Toppings: Banana slices, peanut butter drizzle, dark chocolate chips

Directions:

1. In a large bowl, blend the frozen banana slices, peanut butter, cocoa powder, Greek yogurt, almond milk, and honey or maple syrup until smooth.
2. If necessary, adjust the consistency by adding a little more almond milk, but keep the mixture thick.
3. Transfer the mixture into the CREAMi Pint, ensuring it reaches the MAX Fill line.
4. Secure the lid on the CREAMi Pint and freeze for 24 hours.
5. Once frozen, remove the lid from the CREAMi Pint and place the pint into the Ninja CREAMi.
6. Select the 'Smoothie Bowl' function and process until the mixture is creamy.
7. Serve immediately, garnished with banana slices, a peanut butter drizzle, and a sprinkle of dark chocolate chips.

Nutritional Information (per serving): Protein: 14g | Carbohydrates: 35g | Sodium: 200mg | Potassium: 500mg | Sugar: 30g

Berry Bliss Bowl

Flavor profile: Sweet and slightly tart, bursting with fresh berry flavors.
Best for occasions: Breakfast, Health-Conscious Gatherings

| ❄ Freeze time **24 hours** | 🍲 Prep time **10 minutes** | ⏰ Function time **2 minutes** | ⏲ Servings **4** | 🔥 Calories **140** | Complexity **Beginner** |

Tags: Vegetarian, Refreshing, Creamy, Sweet, Fruity   ***Ninja CREAMi function:*** Smoothie Bowl
Tools needed: Ninja CREAMi, CREAMi Pint, Large Bowl, Spoon, Measuring Cups, Measuring Spoons

Ingredients:

- 2 cups mixed frozen berries (strawberries, blueberries, raspberries)
- 1 cup Greek yogurt
- 1/2 cup almond milk
- 2 tablespoons honey or maple syrup (optional)
- Toppings: Granola, fresh berries, honey drizzle (optional)

Directions:

1. In a large bowl, mix the frozen berries, Greek yogurt, almond milk, and honey or maple syrup until well combined.
2. Adjust the consistency with more almond milk if necessary, ensuring the mixture remains thick.
3. Pour the berry mixture into the CREAMi Pint, filling it to the MAX Fill line.
4. Place the lid on the CREAMi Pint and freeze for 24 hours.
5. After freezing, remove the lid from the CREAMi Pint and insert the pint into the Ninja CREAMi.
6. Select the 'Smoothie Bowl' function and process the mixture until it achieves a smooth, creamy texture.
7. Serve the smoothie bowl in individual bowls, topped with granola, fresh berries, and an additional drizzle of honey if desired.

Nutritional Information (per serving): Protein: 6g | Carbohydrates: 28g | Sodium: 30mg | Potassium: 200mg | Sugar: 27g

Chocoholic's Delight Bowl

Flavor profile: Rich and creamy with a deep peanut butter taste, complemented by sweet banana and a hint of chocolate.
Best for occasions: Health-Conscious Gatherings, Breakfast

❄ Freeze time **24 hours**	Prep time **10 minutes**	Function time **2 minutes**	Servings **4**	Calories **330**	Complexity **Beginner**

Tags: Vegetarian, Refreshing, Creamy, Spiced, Sweet, Nutty   **Ninja CREAMi function:** Smoothie Bowl

Tools needed: Ninja CREAMi, CREAMi Pint, Large Bowl, Spoon, Measuring Cups, Measuring Spoons

Ingredients:

- 2 ripe bananas, sliced and frozen
- 1/2 cup peanut butter
- 2 tablespoons cocoa powder
- 1 cup Greek yogurt
- 1/4 cup almond milk
- 2 tablespoons honey or maple syrup (optional)
- Toppings: Banana slices, peanut butter drizzle, dark chocolate chips

Directions:

1. In a large bowl, blend the frozen banana slices, peanut butter, cocoa powder, almond milk, and honey or maple syrup until smooth.
2. Adjust the consistency with more almond milk if needed, but keep the mixture thick.
3. Transfer the mixture into the CREAMi Pint, filling up to the MAX Fill line.
4. Place the lid on the CREAMi Pint and freeze for 24 hours.
5. Once frozen, remove the lid from the CREAMi Pint and insert the pint into the Ninja CREAMi.
6. Use the 'Smoothie Bowl' function to process until the mixture reaches a creamy texture.
7. Serve immediately, topped with shaved dark chocolate, additional banana slices, and a sprinkle of cocoa nibs.

Nutritional Information (per serving): Protein: 14g | Carbohydrates: 35g | Sodium: 200mg | Potassium: 500mg | Sugar: 30g

---

Zesty Mango-Lime Bowl

Flavor profile: Bright and zesty with the sweetness of mango balanced by the sharpness of fresh lime.
Best for occasions: Summer Gatherings, Health-Conscious Gatherings

❄ Freeze time **24 hours**	Prep time **10 minutes**	Function time **2 minutes**	Servings **4**	Calories **120**	Complexity **Beginner**

Tags: Vegetarian, Refreshing, Creamy, Sweet, Tangy   **Ninja CREAMi function:** Smoothie Bowl

Tools needed: Ninja CREAMi, CREAMi Pint, Large Bowl, Spoon, Measuring Cups, Measuring Spoons

Ingredients:

- 2 cups frozen mango chunks
- 1 ripe banana, sliced
- Juice of 2 limes
- Zest of 1 lime
- 1/4 cup coconut water
- Toppings: Lime zest, sliced mango, toasted coconut flakes

Directions:

1. In a large bowl, mix the frozen mango chunks, sliced banana, lime juice, and half of the lime zest. Stir until well combined.
2. Gradually add coconut water, adjusting the consistency to ensure the mixture is slightly fluid but still thick.
3. Pour the mixture into the CREAMi Pint, ensuring it reaches the MAX Fill line.
4. Secure the lid on the CREAMi Pint and freeze for 24 hours.
5. After freezing, remove the lid from the CREAMi Pint and insert the pint into the Ninja CREAMi.
6. Select the 'Smoothie Bowl' function and process until the mixture is creamy.
7. Serve immediately, garnished with additional lime zest, sliced mango, and toasted coconut flakes.

Nutritional Information (per serving): Protein: 2g | Carbohydrates: 28g | Sodium: 5mg | Potassium: 250mg | Sugar: 27g

Exotic Dragon Bowl

Flavor profile: Sweet and tropical with a distinct dragon fruit flavor, complemented by the lushness of mango.
Best for occasions: Summer Gatherings, Kids' Fun Day

| ❄ Freeze time **24 hours** | 🍲 Prep time **15 minutes** | ⏰ Function time **2 minutes** | 🕐 Servings **4** | 🔥 Calories **150** | ⚊⚊ Complexity **Beginner** |

Tags: Vegetarian, Refreshing, Creamy, Sweet, Fruity   ***Ninja CREAMi function:*** Smoothie Bowl
Tools needed: Ninja CREAMi, CREAMi Pint, Large Bowl, Spoon, Measuring Cups, Measuring Spoons

Ingredients:

- 1 large dragon fruit, pureed
- 1 cup frozen mango chunks
- 1 ripe banana, sliced
- 1/2 cup coconut milk
- Toppings: Kiwi slices, dragon fruit chunks, coconut flakes

Directions:

1. In a large bowl, combine the dragon fruit puree, frozen mango chunks, sliced banana, and coconut milk. Stir well to create a smooth mixture.
2. If the mixture is too thick, adjust the consistency by adding a bit more coconut milk.
3. Pour the mixture into the CREAMi Pint, filling up to the MAX Fill line.
4. Secure the lid on the CREAMi Pint and freeze for 24 hours.
5. After freezing, remove the lid from the CREAMi Pint and insert the pint into the Ninja CREAMi.
6. Process using the 'Smoothie Bowl' function until the mixture reaches a creamy consistency.
7. Serve the smoothie bowl immediately, garnished with kiwi slices, dragon fruit chunks, and coconut flakes.

Nutritional Information (per serving): Protein: 2g | Carbohydrates: 28g | Sodium: 15mg | Potassium: 350mg | Sugar: 27g

CONCLUSION

As we conclude this festive journey with the Ninja CREAMi Culinary Adventures Cookbook's Christmas Edition, we hope that it has inspired you to create heartwarming homemade frozen treats in your kitchen. This book was crafted to be both a guide and an inspiration, illustrating the boundless possibilities that your Ninja CREAMi enables during the holiday season.

Within these pages, you've discovered recipes ranging from holiday classics to exciting new creations, all made possible with the Ninja CREAMi. Whether you've prepared a batch of rich eggnog ice cream, a tart cranberry sorbet, a creamy peppermint gelato, or a spiced pumpkin smoothie bowl, each recipe offered a chance to delve into new flavors and textures reflective of the yuletide spirit.

Remember, the journey doesn't end here. The world of frozen desserts is vast and ever-evolving, and your Ninja CREAMi is the perfect companion to experiment and innovate with festive flair. We encourage you to continue exploring, adjusting, and inventing. Use the skills and knowledge you've gathered from this book as a springboard for your culinary creativity during the holidays and beyond.

Thank you for choosing the Ninja CREAMi Culinary Adventures Cookbook's Christmas Edition as your guide. May your kitchen echo with laughter, your bowls overflow with delectable treats, and your hearts swell with the joy of sharing these delightful desserts with loved ones. Keep churning, smiling, and, most importantly, savoring the sweet moments.

Happy CREAMi Adventures and Merry Christmas!

APPENDIX. MEASUREMENT CONVERSIONS CHART

Liquid Volume Conversions

US Measurements	Metric Measurements	US Standard (Ounces)
1 teaspoon (tsp)	4.93 milliliters (mL)	0.1666 fluid ounces
1 tablespoon (tbsp)	14.79 milliliters (mL)	0.5 fluid ounces
1 fluid ounce (fl oz)	29.57 milliliters (mL)	1 fluid ounce
1 cup (c)	237 milliliters (mL)	8 fluid ounces
1 pint (pt)	473 milliliters (mL)	16 fluid ounces
1 quart (qt)	0.95 liters (L)	32 fluid ounces
1 gallon (gal)	3.79 liters (L)	128 fluid ounces

Dry Weight Conversions

US Measurements	Metric Measurements
1 ounce (oz)	28.35 grams (g)
1 pound (lb)	0.45 kilograms (kg)

INDEX

L

Lemon Custard Gelato, 65
Lite and Dairy-free Ice cream, 45

M

Mango Passion Fruit Sorbet, 58
Mango Tango Lite Ice Cream, 46
Matcha Green Tea Ice Cream, 34
Mince Pie Lite Ice Cream, 23
Mint Chocolate Chip Gelato, 69
Mojito Lime Sorbet, 63
Mojito Sorbet, 39
Mulled Wine Sorbet, 24

N

New Year's Eve Berry Sorbet, 29

O

Orange Blossom Gelato, 68

P

Peach and Prosecco Gelato, 67
Peanut Butter Dream Bowl, 71
Pear Ginger Sorbet, 62
Pecan Pie Ice Cream, 38
Peppermint Mocha Milkshake, 17
Piña Colada Milkshake, 57
Pistachio & Cherry Gelato, 22
Pumpkin Spice Smoothie Bowl, 27

R

Raspberry & Mint Ice Cream, 32
Raspberry Lemonade Bowl, 71
Raspberry Rose Sorbet, 59
Raspberry White Chocolate Gelato, 64
Red Velvet Ice Cream, 33
Roasted Chestnut Gelato, 28

S

Salted Caramel & Pecan Ice Cream, 37
S'mores Ice Cream, 44
Spiced Chai Ice Cream, 35
Spiced Orange and Cranberry Ripple Ice Cream, 27
Spiced Pear Cider Sorbet, 20
Strawberry Cheesecake Milkshake, 54
Strawberry Coconut Dairy-Free Ice Cream, 47

T

Toffee Nut Latte Milkshake 25
Tropical Sunrise Bowl, 70

V

Vegan Chocolate Peanut Butter Milkshake, 56

W

Watermelon Mint Sorbet, 60
White Chocolate Raspberry Ice Cream, 41
Winter Spice Apple Gelato, 21

Y

Yuletide Orange Chocolate Ice Cream, 23

Z

Zesty Mango-Lime Bowl, 73

Made in the USA
Las Vegas, NV
09 January 2025